AWESOME

D1320580

YOUTH

SUNDAYS

BY MARTHA JOHNSON

Bridge Resources
Louisville, Kentucky

Edited by Beth Basham
Book interior and cover design by Pip Pullen
Illustrations by Shawn Lee

First edition

Bridge Resources
Louisville, Kentucky

PRINTED IN THE UNITED STATES OF AMERICA

CONTENTS

The Book in Brief iv

1 Stumbling onto Youth Sunday 1

2 What Makes a Youth Sunday Service Work? 5

3 Picking a Theme 10

4 Research and Brainstorming that Young People Can Do 13

5 The General Order of Service 17

6 The Script, Props, and Bulletin 24

The Services

7 Walls 27

8 Water 49

9 Feet 68

10 Wheat 85

11 Swords 99

12 Wind 113

13 Blood (includes communion service) 130

The Author . . . . Inside back cover

Awesome Youth Sundays lays out a creative process and seven examples of scripts for gutsy and satisfying worship services. Based on the author's experiences with the youth groups of the First Presbyterian Church of Annapolis, Maryland, the book tells of turning a floundering event into the centerpiece of a church youth program.

The first half of the book is devoted to the philosophy (and tricks) that Johnson and the young people evolved to energize their preparations and services. She begins with a process for choosing a

THE BOOK IN BRIEF

concrete, one-word theme such as "Water" or "Swords," full of biblical symbolism and modern meaning. She explains a subsequent research process in which the young people learn about a concordance to the Bible and the hymnbook. Walking the reader through a basic Order of Service, she reveals the potential in each section for the youth to find new meaning and expression within the rituals. She also explains the disciplines of group brainstorming and the wonderful creativity it evokes.

The second half is given over to scripts of seven worship services: Walls, Water, Feet, Wheat, Swords, Wind, and Blood. In each script the reader finds dozens of ideas:

▼ a burning bush brought alive by a tight circle of dancers madly waving flame-colored scarves

▼ a sermon on the children of Somalia, Bosnia, the streets of America, and of God—and where their bread comes from

▼ a rap on Noah and the perils of water

▼ a "flip book" that turns swords into plowshares

▼ the story of the loaves and fishes explained by passing out handfuls of fish-shaped oyster crackers

▼ a frame at the sanctuary entrance that acts as a "metal detector" for those entering the sanctuary for the Swords service

▼ pinwheels on Wind Sunday replacing flowers in the altar vases

▼ and much more

The reader is also provided with a list of props and paraphernalia and a sample bulletin and cover for each service.

More than anything, *Awesome Youth Sundays* offers the reader a vision of moving, involving, and intergenerational worship experiences. Johnson and the youth had a great time immersing themselves in substantive worship events.

So can you.

In years past, January meant a queasy, carsick feeling for everyone in our church youth program. As we headed around the bend on the winter calendar, Youth Sunday loomed on the horizon.

Our church, the Presbyterian Church (U.S.A.), traditionally observes an annual Youth Sunday. Usually we follow the standard Presbyterian Church (U.S.A.) calendar for the service. There, Youth Sunday tends to fall in the busy spring graduation season. The junior high (sixth through eighth grade) and senior high (ninth through twelfth grade) youth groups are given the run of the service. They decide what to do, choose the music, make the bulletins, and lead the service. The youth advisers plan, facilitate, and generally shepherd the process.

CHAPTER 1

Our story is not unique. In many ways, Youth Sunday was a big headache. It competed for time and attention with the slew of activities that mark our congregation's year. Occasionally someone poured in enthusiasm and energy and polished it up. But otherwise it usually just bumped along—never expecting or reaching brilliance. Our church's culture is a kind one, but does not set a high bar of challenge for the young people. We didn't ask much, and we didn't get much.

Many of the problems we faced might sound familiar to other youth leaders. We had no premium on talent. We had no particular head start in resources. Does any of this sound familiar?

ANXIETY AND STRESS

A youth-led worship service is an event. While it is not a theater production or a homecoming parade, it does involve a deadline, an hour to fill, and an expectant congregation. That's enough intensity for any collection of youth leaders.

One year our principal Youth Sunday adult adviser landed in the hospital with appendicitis the day before the service. She carried the script in her head. We were quite dependent on her energy and organizational drive. With her removed from the scene, we had to scramble.

We realized more acutely than ever how thin our ranks and confidence were. The youth advisers typically faced the experience by drinking gallons of coffee and pitching their voices up three notches. We shouted even more that year.

LACK OF RESOURCES

Even if your church has the luxury of a dedicated staffer for youth programs, which we did not, it is not a small task to unearth quality materials. Finding something contemporary and worshipful for an hour-long service is a stretch. Good "canned services" are rarely that good and require extensive reworking to fit the setting and needs of a particular congregation.

THE CONTENT

Congregations are well intentioned but often slow to be in touch with youth culture. Ours was no exception. Youth language, style, and even posture is at times hard to reconcile with a sanctuary experience. Getting the youth excited about the meaning and purpose of the service requires a certain boldness and courage by the youth advisers. What ideas and issues will work? How do the youth advisers balance what is appropriate with what is real for the youth?

UNEXCITING RESULTS

Our services were uneven at best. Sometimes they resembled talent shows. Sometimes they were skits with recycled Christmas costumes and once even with chicken-wire vegetables. While fun, they were frankly banal. We worshiped God by admiring the antics of our children.

MINIMAL LEARNING BY THE YOUTH

Like others, we sometimes fell back on camplike vespers. Often a folk-style touch was created by guitars and musical rounds. This offered the boomers in the church, who are now parents, a sense of nostalgia. The youth, however, got off easy. They rarely learned much of substance or grappled with serious forms of expression. What they got was a replay of summer camp.

THE IDEA GOT LOST

Our Youth Sunday services also felt a bit painful. Some of the young people were nervous. Some were show-offs. Some were embarrassed and couldn't (or wouldn't) project their voices. Prayers were read at breakneck speed. Frankly, everyone loves the *idea* of the youth doing the service, but in fact the event was mostly elbows and awkward moments.

If any of these afflictions visit themselves on your congregation's efforts to have youth develop and lead worship, feel comforted. We have been there. Somehow, it was in our malaise that we stumbled forward and finally stumbled onto a new path. We hope our story and ideas can be of use to you and the blessed work of youth ministry.

Though our services were developed for a designated "Youth Sunday," these services can be used at any time throughout the year.

WE GOT LUCKY (A YOUTH TO THE RESCUE, OF COURSE!)

We remember well when we finally hit pay dirt. It was one dark and stormy February night, and we knew we were already late in planning the annual service. Of course we were doing everything we could to avoid the inevitable. After potluck dinner, we collapsed in the youth room and wasted time chuckling over the memories of the cheers and skits used the year before.

Finally we started to talk about what had happened in the last year. It had been a big news year (1989–90 and the Berlin Wall), and we all sensed that we could not ignore it. Brainstorming sessions have a way of being stalled, and then when frustration peaks, the idea comes. It was like that.

We went round and round with long pauses and dumb ideas when suddenly someone said, "Let's do 'Walls'!" It was as if our car scraped bottom on a sleepy country drive. We jolted awake.

Everyone had ideas.

The first thing we did was assign Jericho to the junior highs. "That gets them out of our hair," said one senior high.

Someone suggested scenery that looked like the Berlin Wall. An adult talked about his memories of the Iron Curtain speech. We thought about people who died trying to escape from East Berlin. We began listing hymns that would work, and "A Mighty Fortress Is Our God" came immediately to mind. We decided to use newspaper headlines about Mandela's release on the bulletin cover. And on and on.

Everyone found it easy to get excited and involved. Parents built a hinged, four panel backdrop that we have used since. Youth fretted over costumes. We argued about the light in the sanctuary. The rappers started tapping and beating rhythms on anything in sight (heads included). The advisers felt focused and reasonably in control. One family made plans to tape the service.

Needless to say, the service was brilliant and stunning. The youth were thrilled. The adults were delighted. The single idea of "Walls" had brought everyone together successfully. The content was gripping; the biblical connections powerful. We were rewarded for our firm belief in the efficacy of elemental and simple ideas. You can get a taste of the service later in this book.

The next spring our nerves started to jangle again. Although we knew we had a good thing, we didn't quite trust it. The theme, "Walls," felt so appropriate and important for 1990, but we weren't sure our formula would work again the next year.

But we need not have been so anxious about repeating our success. In 1991 we again hit on the right theme: "Water." It resonated with our experiences as a Navy town, the recent Gulf War, and great biblical symbolism. Our process began to take clearer form. The service started to fuse into a routine. Little rituals started to take hold. The singing was great. We were hooked. The congregation began to anticipate and understand what we were doing. They became more involved. More people attended the services.

We have now done seven services: Walls, Water, Feet, Wheat, Swords, Wind, and Blood. Each has been special in its own way, created out of the events of our time. We have found our stride. Although we have a formula of sorts, each service has been a unique gem.

Youth advisers have come and gone. We have learned that our process and core ideas have translated easily to new leaders. Each has picked up the effort and found it possible to own the template and gear up the young people. We should be able to continue building on our experiences and deepening our traditions.

This staying power has convinced us that we have something to explain and share with others. We decided to write it all down. We hope our ideas can spur you forward on your road. Godspeed.

We never wondered hard about what made our services tick. They just did. The reasons and the "formula" seemed obvious. The services emerged so naturally from the group that we were not conscious of their defining value or the uniqueness of the process. Things always jelled, and that was enough for us.

It has been hard to step back and dissect our repeated success. It is like explaining how to breathe or sing. As we think about it, though, a half dozen hooks stick out. We were lucky to have grabbed on to them so effortlessly.

CHAPTER 2

Little did we appreciate how the synergy occurred until we explored it for this book. Because of this, we feel the process can be just as natural and organic for others. Although we parse our process for the reader in a linear and deliberate way and make it sound like a very conscious effort to undertake, we believe it will quickly gain its own natural creative life for you too.

CHOOSE A THEME

Our core trick is to create a service around a concrete, one-word theme. Choosing our own theme is a slight rebellion. We have not yet been convinced to use the lectionary for the designated Sunday. Neither have we relied on suggested Youth Sunday topics by the denominational offices. The theme has always emerged naturally out of the events of the year and the passions of the group.

Once the theme is chosen, we suggest the group bring everything to bear on it: music, spoken word, costumes, dress, drama, decorations, dance, rituals, seating arrangements, bulletins, lighting, and anything else that pertains to the time and space of the worship hour.

Starting with a clear and definable theme keeps everyone focused. It forces a single direction and asserts a form of coherence and control that everyone recognizes—and remembers. Years later people will remember the "Wind" year or the "Gold" service.

The theme also eliminates the hard parts, the early stewing and anxiety associated with trying to figure out what to do. We often think of it as a compass needle—fastened down at the center but capable of spinning in any direction. Yet we have never spun out of control.

FOLLOW A BASIC ORDER OF SERVICE

Use a General Order of Service each year. This might seem obvious but it should not be ignored. In some religious traditions a particular order of service is expected. Having such a template takes away most of the early *Sturm und Drang*. By sticking to the same order, the group can pour energy into the individual parts of the service. Clarifying the high-level script lightens everyone's burdens.

ESTABLISH SIMPLE RITUALS

Accidently, in our first service we did a few things that we repeated the next year. Soon these became important though small rituals. They eased our writing and creative tasks over time. For example, we fell into the habit of asking the younger children of the church (fourth- and fifth-graders) to collect the offering. They now expect to be asked. It is a rite of passage to do the offering before you get to be *in* Youth Sunday. This builds up the excitement and involvement for more of the congregation.

As another example, we include a section called "Time with Adults." This is a little joke. It is a sermon-minor that is fashioned on the "Time with Children" or "Children's Sermon" slot in our regular Sunday service.

A third ritual is a responsive benediction. The youth gather at the front of the sanctuary and begin with a few lines: "And now go forth . . . " The congregation answers, " . . . May God bless you, children, and be with you." The youth conclude with "And with you, too, O children of God." It is a lovely and innocent charge that leaves the congregation awash in emotion and the youth jubilant that they have made it through another service.

USE THE "WHOLE KEYBOARD"

Aim to challenge and involve people with all their senses, in all the space you have, with every art form you can muster. Remember, however, this is not an exercise in Disney-styled pyrotechnics. Fancy or elaborate does not equal effective. Gestures and embellishments can be *very, very* simple and still add immeasurably to the hearing or speaking of a message. Play the whole keyboard, not just the singable keys. And keep an ear out for cacophony.

There is unending scope. Here are some options:

Spatial
Use the aisles, altar rail, altar table, balcony, choir loft, curtains, doors, entrance, lectern, lighting fixtures, molding, pews, pew racks, pulpit, steps, walls, windows.

Pay attention to your church layout. Is it a center-aisle sanctuary or in the round? Is it large or intimate? Where might people sit and in what arrangements?

Sounds
Use music, finger snapping, feet tapping, clapping, hissing, humming, moaning, single voices, echoes (repeating the last word or phrase), antiphonal (two or more people placed in different parts of the sanctuary and reading in turns), sound ranges (rough and loud to sweet and melodic), percussion (drums, cymbals, triangles, gongs, bongos, tambourines). Have a town crier make announcements in a loud voice, announced by a bell.

Sing hymns by gender—males on one stanza, females on the next. Read the same biblical passage from a variety of Bibles. Read or sing in different languages.

Actions
Try hand washing, feet washing, hanging memorial crosses, baton twirling, guided breathing and imaging, twirling in the aisles, individually composed prayers, congregational waves, stomping to certain rhythms, going barefoot, opening or closing doors, curtains, or windows.

Ask the whole congregation to process during the first hymn. Invite the congregation to gather in a large circle around the sanctuary for the Prayers of the People.

Sing hymns by gender—males on one stanza, females on the next. Read the same biblical passage from a variety of Bibles. Read or sing in different languages. Go barefoot. Twirl in the aisles. Rope off sections of the sanctuary and forbid people to sit there.

Decorations or Other Props
Distribute or display flags, flowers, fans, bookmarks, streamers, banners, pinwheels, balloons, bouquets of grains or foods, ribbons, painted backdrop, relevant collections.

Color
Use all one color (clothes, decorations, flowers, balloons) or a variety of colors against a common background color.

Storytelling
Use puppets, dance, various hats, shadow images, large figures (made out of clothing stuffed with newspaper or straw), paper images attached to ends of poles.

EMBRACE JUXTAPOSITIONS

The obvious nature of the service is a juxtaposition; the youth are doing what grown-ups usually handle. This enlivens and sharpens worship. Another important juxtaposition is to draw on both the Bible and contemporary events. The juxtapositions can be very simple and subtle. Review the service and see if it has developed or taken advantage of any others.

Expected/Unexpected
Begin the service with a routine processional (expected); deliver the filled offering plates to the front by skipping down the aisle (unexpected). *Don't spill.*

Guided/Free
Follow a responsive prayer with a moment of silence during which people are invited to voice individual prayers.

Orderly/Random
The choir stands in traditional lines for one anthem and then in scattered formation for another.

Together/Personal
Use a whole loaf when exploring a story and then distribute crackers. Enjoy a bouquet of balloons and then pass them out. Sing in unison and then listen to a solo.

PLACE EXPECTATIONS ON THE YOUTH

Placing expectations on the youth means the difference between a service that fills an hour and one that has life beyond it. Having a theme and a tight structure allows extra psychic energy necessary to put expectations and assignments on the youth and see them through.

We usually have to search for a balance. Young people are extremely busy and over-scheduled these days. Giving them appropriately challenging parts is important, nevertheless. For some youth, simply reading Scriptures is tough sledding. Finding parts that make them stretch but allow them to shine is critical. For the more poised and capable, doing something with expression, finesse, or good timing is the challenge. Learning can involve much more than memorizing parts. The wonderful thing about a service is there is room for a wide range of abilities and confidence.

ADOPT A MULTIYEAR APPROACH

Usually when Youth Sunday preparations are under way, the single thought in everyone's mind is to get through the service alive. Try to be more expansive. In fact, it is easy to begin to build tradition. This need not be restrictive. There is little that is so special it must be obliged year in and year out. A loose rhythm, a couple of simple structures, an attitude that the youth will be with you each year and carrying something forward each time can make all the difference.

SAFETY

This might sound odd. However, a successful Youth Sunday service is one in which a congregation can quickly adjust and, therefore, participate. This requires a good balance between those things that are new, experimental, spontaneous, unsettling, or challenging, and those that anchor and "keep" the congregation with you. That is safety. In a safe environment, people can feel secure that they will not be embarrassed, lost, or made to feel foolish. The norms can be moved but should not be violated.

The underlying philosophy here is important. Worship is a time for personal *and* corporate stretching and reaching to God. Therefore worship requires juggling freedom and convention so that it provides: (a) an immediacy and spontaneity in which individuals can each find an avenue for meaning and personal experience, and (b) structures so that everyone understands some basic rules and can participate in a corporate, group venture.

A worship service with too much of A and not enough of B does not meet people's needs. And the same in reverse. A service, particularly a youth-created service, can easily err on the first and overstep the lines of safety. To head this off, a clear theme and a set of familiar forms gives the congregation an anchor of familiarity. The safety of people knowing what and how they will share together keeps everyone secure, focused, and engaged.

It can be difficult to find this balance, especially when a service steps outside normal patterns. Using a clear, uniting theme helps. Picking up a few rituals over the years helps. Using the organ for the first hymn helps. With a clear beat and an audible bass, an organ creates a sense of order without imposing a sense of control.

The process of building the service also establishes this balance. First we strip down to the basic order of service. And then we construct. We reduce the service to a familiar skeleton: a single theme, the language of music and Scripture. With those essentials we then release our imaginations.

Of course, everyone has extra grace to offer for Youth Sunday. People know a service run by the young people will be different, perhaps startling, and outside the routine. There is plenty of room in everyone's hearts to flex those young and creative muscles and share a service filled with strength, substance, and beauty.

The single core task in making Youth Sunday a successful creative experience is to pick a theme. The theme acts as a frame for the entire service. It also acts as a springboard for the developing, writing, and imagining process ahead. The rules for a theme are simple:

The theme is *one* word, a noun, preferably something you can see and touch.

The theme works best if it

CHAPTER 3

▼ is universal, common to human experience (water, apple, stone, fish)

▼ has biblical life (do not pick computers or telephones)

▼ evokes stories out of the past year's events: international, national, regional, local, congregational, personal

▼ lends itself to symbolism

Themes are most successful if you do the following:

▼ *Avoid* choosing a *conceptual* noun: mission, love, faith, mercy, passion, forgiveness, hope, resurrection, grace, communion, creation

▼ *Avoid* choosing obviously *religious* words: cross, Bible, pulpit, altar, sermon, prayer, steeple, rosary, missionary

This might sound sacrilegious to some. Let me explain. The power of any worship service comes from strong symbolism and allusion. People gather spiritual strength from new connections between the everyday or mundane and the sacred. Choosing a plain or simple object heightens the miracle of the connection with the sacred. Choosing a concept or philosophical idea does not offer much to work with visually nor does it allow for that unexpected and delightful connection.

Likewise, choosing a religious object does not offer the opportunity to point up the distance and immediacy of the simple and the sacred.

Besides, youth get a kick out of an object theme. They seem to enjoy and catch on to the wonder of finding the rings of meaning and ritual that something simple can produce.

TASK ONE: AGREEING ON A THEME

The process of choosing a theme should start early. It is the first task in preparing for Youth Sunday.

Process

1. Start by making a long list of ideas. Kick off with a suggested list on a flip chart of about five to ten ideas (use any or none of the ones listed at the end

of the chapter.) Urge the youth to think of current events or things that happened in the course of the year. Then just ask them to list ideas as fast as they can with no comments about whether an idea is good or bad.

2. When you have generated enough ideas, call a halt to the brainstorming. Start to pare down the list. Cross off duplications and themes that were in last year's category. Talk about the merits of each one.

3. A theme needs to open doors for the group. A good service builds from a rich abundance of material. The theme needs to set that up. To test a theme try asking the following questions:

▼ Does everyone (adults *and* children) know this word?

▼ Can it be represented by a simple drawing?

▼ What colors come to mind when you think of this theme?

▼ What music, songs, hymns, or recordings include this theme?

▼ Does a Bible concordance have a long entry for the theme?

▼ Does it appear in the Bible in different places?

▼ Are there multiple citations for the theme both in the Old Testament and in the New Testament?

▼ Is it associated with a variety of biblical stories, events, parables, or other situations?

▼ Can we have fun with this theme?

▼ What events of the past year involved, contained, or included this theme? Think broadly across the news and events.

▼ How significant is the event?

▼ How familiar is the event?

▼ Do we want to devote some time in the service to it?

▼ What associations does the theme suggest? (e.g., the theme Feet reminds us of paths, walking, journeys, roads, shoes, hands)

▼ Are any of these associations in the Bible?

▼ Who cares about this theme?

Take time with these questions. Mulling over a theme in this manner will begin to give you ideas for material for the service. Have someone take notes during the discussion. The discussion will build important consensus. Surprisingly, the youth develop great allegiance to the theme. Keep talking. Use judgment. Eventually one will feel broader, richer, and more relevant than the others. It is worth the effort early on to nail down everyone's agreement and comfort with the theme.

Sample Themes

Note: The more immediate or specific the theme, the better. Avoid choosing a category such as "furniture." Choose instead a specific piece of furniture such as a table, bed, or chair.

Category: Animals

Themes: bird, donkey, dove, eagle, fish, goat, horse, lamb, lion, locust, ox, pigeon, ram, raven, sheep, snake, whale

Category: Body Parts

Themes: ears, eyes, face, feet, hands, head, heart, knees, mouth, shoulder, skin, stomach

Category: Buildings

Themes: bricks, walls, windows, doors, stairs, furnace, room, roof, porch, garden, gate, barns, wells, house, city, market, prison, palace

Category: Clothing/adornment

Themes: veil, shoes, robe, crown, mantel, sandals, perfume, ring, coat

Category: Furniture

Themes: lamp, chair, table, jar/urn, throne, cup, bed, curtain

Category: Food

Themes: wheat, wine, apple, fish, grapes, honey

Category: Musical Instruments

Themes: harp, bell, drum, flute, cymbal, trumpet/horn, gong

Category: Nature

Themes: sand, mud, stone, straw, water, seed, leaves, flower, vine, branch, twig, bush, cedar, palm, oak, tree, fire, smoke, brook, river, stream, coast, valley, forest, cave, mountain, lake, ocean, star, sun

Category: People

Themes: daughter, son, baby, maid, servant, giant, king, prostitute, fisherman, steward, prophet, mason, sailor, farmer, fool, lord, stranger

Category: Things/Paraphernalia

Themes: rope, sword, chain, book, box, cloth, basket, blankets, ointment, pot

Category: Tools

Themes: shovel, ax, hoe, knife, hammer

Category: Transportation

Themes: chariot, cart, wagon, path, road, sign, boat, sail, ship

Category: Wealth

Themes: oil, gold, money, purse, jewels, ring

Category: Weather

Themes: wind, hail, rain, thunder, clouds

RESEARCH AND BRAINSTORMING THAT
YOUNG PEOPLE CAN DO

With the theme chosen, Youth Sunday is well on its way. The next project is to scan the world for anything that even hints at the theme. From this large body of ideas you can choose the best material for the service.

TASK ONE: BUILDING SKILLS

In this session, youth will be given the opportunity to develop valuable skills, namely, using a concordance to the Bible, the hymnbook and other songbooks, as well as participating in disciplined brainstorming sessions.

CHAPTER 4

The concordance is easy because topics are listed alphabetically. Underneath each is a full listing of every use of a topic word in the Bible. Youth can then flip through their Bibles and see if those listings are useful or catchy for a service.

The hymnbook is also easy but requires that you take a few moments to show them the "map." Often youth do not know there is an index of titles, one of scriptural allusions, a topical listing, and an index of the first line of each song. In addition, point out the metrical list. When they understand that hymns with the same metrics can swap words and tunes, they might want to choose an unfamiliar set of lyrics and plan to use a familiar tune for it.

Formal brainstorming is a little more foreign to most. The rules are not hard, and even advisers often need to review them.

Process

1. Pose the clear question: "What does the theme, _____, remind you of?" or "What could we do with the theme, _____, in the service?"

2. Ask a scribe to quickly write down every idea that is offered. Use felt-tipped markers and flip charts so all can see. Nothing is too silly or esoteric to be ignored.

3. Ask that no one be allowed to make *any* kind of comment on another person's idea—either critical or funny. This is important because people can immediately feel group censorship. The facilitator must work deliberately to create this process in which ideas can flow freely and creatively.

4. Brainstorm about the ideas listed. The brainstorming session must be run with a clear time frame. Indicate when it starts and when it will stop and stick to that. This little bit of pressure somehow induces more creativity than one would expect.

5. Finally, silence is golden. If people run out of ideas, don't stop the session. Let the silence exist.

Note: Task One is detailed in Chapter 3, "Picking a Theme."

TASK TWO: DEVELOPING THE MESSAGE WITH A CONCORDANCE OF THE BIBLE

In the next youth-gathering time, place the youth in small groups and give each group a concordance of the Bible.

Process

1. Take a moment to show them how it works.

2. Ask youth to make a list of Bible verses that relate to the chosen theme.

3. Write them legibly on a flip chart.

4. List both the citation and a quick reminder of the words or message.

This can fill an hour or more if done thoroughly. Aim to be as comprehensive as possible.

TASK THREE: DEVELOPING THE MESSAGE WITH THE MUSIC

Next, hand out piles of hymnbooks and songbooks.

Process

1. Ask youth to browse through the books and scout out music that reminds them of the theme. Allow some time for this exercise. Remind them to scan both the song titles in the index *and* the lyrics of songs in the body of the book.

2. Make a list of songs that relate. Write them legibly on a flip chart.

It is easy to spot directly related hymn and song titles. However, the lyrics are equally powerful though may be less obvious. Don't let youth ignore these hymns. For example:

Theme	Lyrics
Wheat	Let Us Break Bread Together
Wind	Breathe on Me, Breath of God
Arms	Our God, Our Help in Ages Past—"Sufficient is thine arm alone . . ."
	Eternal Father, Strong to Save "Whose arm has bound the restless wave . . ."

TASK FOUR: DEVELOPING THE MESSAGE WITH SECULAR MATERIALS

Begin by getting everyone in a group. Have an adult be the scribe and catch ideas as they are voiced.

Process

1. Ask everyone to think about the year's events and start listing them on the flip chart. Take them through categories: weather, sports, politics, business, entertainment, international events (suggest continents systematically and then major countries). Give everyone time. Don't rush. See how much everyone already knows.

2. Pass out stacks of magazines and have the group flip through and pull out anything that reminds them of the theme: pictures, articles, book reviews, crossword puzzles, comics. Tape these to a flip-chart sheet so everyone can see all the ideas spread out on the walls.

   Youth can get pretty silly doing this. That's OK because they will relax and then their thinking is freed up. Keep steering them back to the scanning work. Don't criticize or "cut" an idea at this point. Simply gather every single thing you can. Aim for quantity.

3. Hang all the research lists on the wall around the room. Cover the walls. Assure yourself that you have more than enough to fashion a service. Go back for more if you do not.

TASK FIVE: SLOTTING MATERIALS INTO THE ORDER OF SERVICE

This section can be done with the group or can be done by an adviser or other adult.[1] You will need the Order of Service commonly used in your church. (See chapter 5.)

Process

1. On an easel pad, title each sheet with a part of the service (e.g., Processional Hymn, Old Testament Reading). If working with a group, appoint a scribe or two.

2. Ask everyone to look at the lists on the walls, and call out ideas, music, Bible selections that would work for various parts of the service. This is a matching process. Try to group similar or connected thoughts into the sermon.

The service requires coherence and flow. Think about the whole service and where it is aiming. The facilitator or scribes need to be steering this thought process. This is a challenge for a group but can be done with thoughtful, concentrated, and guided conversation. One word of caution: You need not use every idea. You might have to eliminate a cherished one. The result should not feel like a scrambled catchall.

---

1. Frankly, we usually assign this work to an adult. If one person tackles the flow of the content of the script, the service gains in coherency, and the process is more efficient.

TASK SIX: MAKING IT COME ALIVE

Once the ideas and the Order of Service are matched up, the fun can begin. With the right content in the right section of the service the group can now create ways to express and share the message.

Task Six should be devoted to formal brainstorming. Follow the rules, and the service will begin to come alive.

Process

1. Begin with any particular section of the service. Explain by asking the question:

> "For part of the service called 'Time with Adults' we want to use the story of _____ from the New Testament. How can we do this?"

The ideas will come slowly at times and then quickly. Give it time and let the quiet times last. You will see ideas build on each other:

"Just read the story."

"Read it while standing on pews in various parts of the congregation."

"Have youth around the sanctuary read the dialogue parts and the narrator stand in the pulpit."

"Make silhouettes of the characters and hold them up around the sanctuary when they 'talk' in the story."

Or ideas might just come at random and even be nonsensical. Let it flow.

Again, no idea is bad; all are welcome.

2. After a number of ideas have been generated, close down the brainstorming. Then talk through which idea has the most excitement, opportunity of action, or creativity, etc. Then move on to another section of the service and so on until you have completed the plan.

The service will begin to have a life of its own. You might decide to make a part of the service very active and unconventional and leave the rest of the service fairly straightforward. Remember there are lots of variables. You want interest in the service; parts for everyone; props that don't exhaust the parents; and a coherent flow. You want everything—and you will get it.

The basic components and order of the service can be easily drawn from the standard framework for the regular Sunday morning service. This template is useful precisely because it is familiar and standard. With all the creativity and special efforts of a youth service, a basic Order of Service minimizes confusion and unnecessary work.

We fall back on our standard framework year after year. It helps us pace the service. It keeps us reasonably organized. It acts as a checklist. It prevents us from either overloading

CHAPTER 5

or underloading the service. We can check that people are signaled to stand or sit at the right times. We can avoid errors such as planningtoo many hymns, forgetting the offering, or allowing lengthy periods when the congregation does not participate.

A template provides some rituals that the youth remember from year to year and anticipate. It also allows us to be flexible without being fragmented. And, of course, if the urge hits, we can stray outside the standard menu. It is not meant to be a constraint as much as a pressure valve, one less aspect of the service that is necessary to grow from seed.

We strongly recommend working from a basic structure. Ours is listed here for your use. Or you can develop one that is more familiar to you or closer to your tradition.

Remember, you need some frame like this for Task Five, which was laid out in the previous chapter.

THE BASIC ELEMENTS

Prelude

Words of Welcome

Call to Worship

Processional Hymn

Unison Prayer (often followed with Response or Words of Assurance)

Gloria Patri

"Time with Adults"

Old Testament Reading

New Testament Reading

Anthem (Hymn)

Meditation/Sermon (in three or more parts)

Hymn

Call to Offering/Offertory/Doxology/Receiving of the Offering

Offering

Prayers of the People

Lord's Prayer

Closing Hymn

Benediction

Postlude

As you work through Task Five of chapter 4, fit material into each section and think about the potential for each part. Here are our thoughts:

Prelude

This section is always left open for the youth to provide the music. Encourage instrumental music rather than solo or small-group singing. Choral lyrics to match the theme are not always easy to find.

Instrumental music is marvelous. Over the years we have had groups of string players, a solo pianist, and even two tubas. Everyone loves to give the youth a chance to perform, and the front of the service is a good time. In the years when no youth is bold or skilled enough to play, we ask the church organist to provide a standard prelude.

In the bulletin under the word "Prelude" we usually insert a biblical verse connected to the service's theme and a brief statement: "While listening to the music of the Prelude, we invite to you consider the following passage: . . ."

Words of Welcome

One or two youth begin the service from the front of the sanctuary, speaking from the lectern or the lectern and the pulpit. When youth read in church they are often hard to listen to: they can rush, whisper, or forget to inflect. To help the congregation hear and understand, the rule of thumb is to limit the reading to two paragraphs. If it is longer, two youth can take turns.

The purpose of this section is to provide a simple context and explanation of the service. We are a downtown church in a tourist community and often have visitors on Sunday morning. The Words of Welcome tell people what they are in for. This is usually evident from the bulletin and the decorations in the church. So it is only fair to help new or irregular attenders feel invited and involved.

Call to Worship

A youth—sometimes two together for volume—read the Call from the back of the church.

The Call is a direct quote from the Bible with perhaps a sentence or two or introduction: As the Lord has said: " . . . "

Processional Hymn

The opening hymn sets the tone for the whole service. It anchors the experience. It signals whether people can trust this time to be a worship service or find themselves watching it as a performance.

Therefore, we always insist on singing a well-known processional hymn with an organ accompaniment. The solid bass of the organ is an important reassurance against the high pitches of the youth voices throughout the service. It steadies everyone to hear that familiar beat. It also relaxes everyone, which is important because many people are anxious. The congregation wants the youth to do well; they want to avoid embarrassment; they want to enjoy and feel involved in the service and not be spectators. Singing a grand hymn together is uniting and uplifting. And the great processional hymns are full of wonderful images that reinforce the service's theme.

We have also had great success in orchestrating the procession more than is customary. The youth process in pairs, keeping three pews apart (otherwise they rush, bunch together, and get distracted). When the first pair reaches the front pews, they stop, and the line of pairs behind them also stops. They turn 90 degrees to face the pews (backs to each other) and continue singing. The congregation enjoys hearing the youth singing closeup. The youth like a little choreography. It adds a sense of elegance. At the beginning of the last verse (or second to last if the verses are short), the youth face forward again and resume the procession to their seats in the choir loft or the front pews.

Unison Prayer (Prayer of Confession; Prayer of Adoration; Prayer of Thanksgiving)

(Often followed with a Response. If the prayer is one of Confession, the Response is called the Words of Assurance.)

This is a short prayer, no more than a standard paragraph. The theme will probably offer a good angle on a prayer and then you can choose what kind of prayer to write.

Gloria Patri

We vacillate between using the standard tune or a livelier, swinging tune. If you use a different tune, be sure to give people notice.

"Time with Adults"

Our regular Sunday morning services have a "Time with Children" or "Children's Sermon." The children gather at the front of the sanctuary where an adult meets them and shares a story or concept with them.

On Youth Sunday the youth like to flip this into a "Time with Adults" for Youth Sunday. It is a little wink in the service. It also allows a clearly designated time in the service for a little zaniness. This has become one of the more cherished moments in the service, and the youth compete to take the assignment. We finally adopted a tradition of letting the seniors have right of first refusal at doing the "Time with Adults."

Usually the entire sermonette is scripted, but the seniors often ad lib the part. It does not always lend itself to being read.

Over the years the youth grow more creative in thinking of the activity. Sometimes their ideas are too wonderful to choose from, so we incorporate the extra ideas into the real sermon. The year we chose the theme "Wind" the youth suggested among other things: (a) fold and shoot paper airplanes with prayers, (b) pass out fire-ball candies (the breath of God), and (c) do a puppet show in which the life-sized (newspaper stuffed) puppet is thrown (blown by the wind) off the altar table behind the choir stalls.

For the Swords service we couldn't choose between two ideas, so we did both. One youth described a collection of toy weapons that were on display (similar to a police display after a weapon raid). We also distributed a "flip book" that showed a picture of a sword turning into a plowshare.

Old Testament Reading

All readings are opportunities to deviate from the norm. The Old Testament Reading can be a time to dramatize, dance, read antiphonally, use puppets, or use "echoes." Particularly when the Scripture includes dialogue, find a way to use more than one voice. A responsive reading with the congregation also keeps everyone involved.

New Testament Reading

The points about Old Testament Readings also apply here.

Anthem

We put an anthem in the service at this point unless we have built music into the Meditations, which come next. We plan for the youth choir to sing rather than invite any solo performances. (We reserve the solos for the Prelude or the Offertory.)

(Hymn)

You can insert another hymn here if you wish, especially if you choose not to have an anthem. We always have three hymns, but a fourth can work. Sometimes the service is just plain short and an extra hymn is nice pacing. Sometimes too many great hymns match the theme and eliminating the fourth is too painful.

Meditation/Sermon (in three or more parts)

The Meditation is the point at which you confront your chosen theme and learn if it has enough depth and weight to sustain an entire service. There should be a good handful—if not lots—of biblical quotes and news items that beg to be stuffed into the sermon.

The Meditation is best if divided into at least three sections. This creates some balance and the opportunity to tackle the theme from a few different angles. Too many sections, though, dilute the individual messages. Often we use music to make transitions inside the Meditation.

Look at your material and see if there are three or so connecting, evolving, or contrasting angles to take. Here are examples of ideas from our services.

Wind

Invites and destroys

Power and nothingness

Endings and beginnings

Water

Destruction

In trouble

Nurture

Redemption

Feet

Forgiveness

Faith

Greed

Celebration

Aim to end on a positive note.

Twice we have written raps as part of the Meditation. This has been relatively easy and a big success. We fall back on a few rules as we write raps. First, we have a general idea of two or three points we want to make. A rap can be embellished with many extra verses that repeat the general idea. It is not necessary to make the rap line for line develop a story line.

Second, make a list of common rhymes with three or four examples of each: rap, sap, cap, lap, map, trap, scrap, etc. (Keep these lists for future "poetry.")

Third, compose a line that ends in one of your standard rhyme words. Then compose another that ends with a rhyme. A rap requires a simple A A B B pattern.

Fourth, use a longer rhythm scheme that allows more rather than less syllables each line. This way you can make more complicated sentences.

Finally, ask for a duo or trio to write a rap. This is a good project and a few people working together can be real innovative, no doubt having heard endless numbers of raps themselves.

Hymn

This is an ideal time to get people to stretch their legs. Never forget to think about the congregation and how to keep them moving and alert.

Call to Offering

One youth stands at the altar table, says a few words, and hands the offering plates to the ushers. This is a good short part for a shy or younger child. Words can be written on a piece of paper placed in the top plate and read inconspicuously.

The ushers can be the younger children of the church (fourth and fifth graders), or the parents. Either is a nice tradition. Offering plates can be modified to reflect the theme (e.g., bread baskets during the Wheat service).

Offertory

A good time for another solo or small musical performance is while the offering is being collected. Like the Prelude, the Offertory can be a solo or small displays of talent without making the service into a concert.

Doxology

As with the Gloria Patri, if you use a different tune, be sure to indicate it in the bulletin. This is the time when the ushers bring the filled plates to the front for a dedication.

Receiving Offering

The offering is dedicated with a few words. Usually the same youth distributes the plates to the ushers and receives and dedicates the offering.

Prayers of the People

We do not usually jazz up this section because the words and thoughts are quite rich enough. However, for the Wind service we asked the youth a month ahead to write prayers on cards. We used those prayers in this section and released a white helium balloon as each one was read. We worried that this would be too trite (balloons are associated with clowns and birthdays). But it turned out to have a simple and earnest feel to it and blended with the theme in a gentle way. We did think about tying little white rags on the strings for each prayer—as the Japanese do outside their temples—but they weighted down the balloons.

When writing the Prayers of the People, try to have a cadence to the prayers to separate the sections. For example, repeat "Be with . . . " at the beginning of each section as we did in the Walls service. Or in the Water service we began each section with a different name for God. In the Feet service we dedicated each section for people who walk differently:

> We pray today for people who walk a path of courage . . .
>
> We pray for those who must walk . . .
>
> We pray for those who cannot walk . . .

Lord's Prayer

The youth who leads the Prayers of the People can conclude them and lead the congregation directly into the Lord's Prayer.

Closing Hymn

The final hymn is usually a recessional hymn, but we script it so that the youth stay in the front and line up on the steps of the chancel. In this position they lead the Benediction.

Benediction

Over the years we have relied on a responsive Benediction:

> Youth: *And now go forth into the world . . .*
>
> Congregation: *Together may we share the light of God's countenance upon us. May God bless you children, and keep you.*
>
> Youth: *And may God bless you, too, O Children of God.*

It is a lovely twist for the children of the church to call the adults "Children of God." It effectively passes the baton back to the adults and concludes Youth Sunday.

Postlude

Because people want to greet the youth immediately, we let the organist play a traditional Postlude. Once we had youth play the Postlude on violins, but the congregation sat back down to listen and the momentum of the closing benediction petered out. Don't be afraid to end the service when it needs to end.

THE SCRIPT

A complete script is the best way to organize, track, and capture for your files the experience of a particular Youth Sunday. Compose the script on a computer so that editing is easy. Date and hand out preliminary copies for early rehearsals. Make thorough notes of any changes, new ideas, repositioning of readers, props needed, and the like. Update and reprint. It is worth the paper.

Give each youth a script (which often even includes the words to the hymns). This will minimize

CHAPTER 6

the amount of stuff each has to juggle during the service. We occasionally take the script, insert the choral music, slap on a construction-paper cover, and staple it all together.

Script out all movement, such as the following:

Sean in pulpit; Katy at lectern.

Laura stands on boxes on the right of the piano.

Jake leaves NOW to get in costume and get to the balcony.

You might find this overly compulsive. It is. But the more you do, the more the youth feel in control. Planning every move also helps the congregation a great deal. Too often they are left standing when they should be seated or unsure if they should listen or join in the music. Make life easy. Tell everyone what to do.

Script out all the words everyone needs to speak (e.g., "Will the congregation please stand"). Doing so helps in surprising ways. Youth feel more secure when they know exactly what to say. Then they can concentrate on speaking clearly. Scripting also shows how much a particular person is expected to speak. It can, therefore, warn you when it is helpful to break up a passage.

Use the words of the Bible as much as possible; they add weight. Using biblical language relieves you of the need to compose a lot. Also, by using biblical passages the youth can focus less on writing and editing the words and more on imagining ways to interpret and express the biblical narration. Turning to the Bible for the dialogue allows you more impunity in the rest of the service. It is a tactic that keeps the congregation comfortable about what the youth are up to. This in turn allows room for other experimenting.

We rarely expect the youth to memorize anything. Occasionally parts such as raps lend themselves to memorization, but those are rare. Avoiding plays or theatrical presentations relieves the youth of learning dialogue. It is enough that the service is largely readings from the Bible and the youth concentrate on remembering what they are supposed to *do* when those words are read.

PROPS, DECORATIONS, COSTUMES, EQUIPMENT

For each of the services included in this book is a section called "Props and Paraphernalia." Start creating a list of props from the very beginning. Some can be made while others need to be collected or bought. Assign craft or construction projects during some fellowship times. This provides a break from the research and writing.

Draw heavily on the young people. Ask them how to display or decorate a passage or prayer. Young people come up with the best ideas. A huge plastic-foam airplane from someone's basement made a debut on a hastily rigged high wire in one service. Put it to them for suggestions.

A backdrop is a wonderful and versatile piece of equipment to have. Our parent group constructed a very sturdy one. We have painted it multiple times and placed it across the front of the chancel. It created quite an effect when we spray-painted large footprints all over the panels. It looked like a mighty fortress when covered with gray stones. The designs on the backdrop have always been very simple, large, and repetitive. We are trying for simplicity when we render a backdrop.

Remember that props can be very simple and still effective. Except for the backdrop, we have always worked within a very frugal budget. We use construction paper, straw, yarn, balloons, pipe cleaners, and other typical arts and crafts items. We aim to create a symbol or illusion of something rather than a realistic presentation. For example, when we used the passage about "all flesh is grass" the youth simply waived long green pipe cleaners.

There is enormous value in thinking about the entrance to the sanctuary and the physical way the theme can be immediately communicated to people as they enter. For the Swords service, we constructed a "metal detector." This was a big frame covered with aluminum foil through which people walked as they entered the sanctuary. For the Feet service we pasted big footprints leading into the church and up the stairs to the sanctuary aisle. Of course, each sanctuary is different, and you will need to make changes depending on your sanctuary's design and floor plan.

Don't ignore the standard decorations and other items of a service. Consider how they could convey the theme.

Flowers
Display clusters of pinwheels, bouquets of wheat stalks.

Offering Plates
Use breadbaskets, water buckets, shoes, cups, soup kitchen pots, recycled machine oil tins, plastic ice cream buckets.

Candles
Use flashlights, camping lanterns, ship lanterns, bedside lamps, create candlesticks made of bricks; use clay to fashion appropriate shapes.

THE BULLETIN

The bulletin for a youth service accomplishes a variety of tasks and should be created with these in mind.

First, the bulletin helps people quickly understand the unique nature of the service. It alerts visitors. It announces that something is up today. People can quickly shift gears and expectations when they read it.

Second, the bulletin helps people listen accurately. To this end, it is longer, giving people more lyrics, explanation, and direction than usual. For example, we print excerpts from hymns so that people quickly connect a hymn with the theme. Whenever we include a rap in the sermon we write it out. When youth are rapping their enunciation falls apart. The youth do their best while the congregation can read along.

Third, the bulletin acquaints the congregation with those involved in the service. It may be hard to list particular youth because assignments change or youth trade parts. Names can be listed next to the more extensive sections such as the sermon. The entire group should be acknowledged at the end.

Fourth, writing the bulletin is easy. It is the last thing to do. Once a full script is written on the computer and finalized, simply save it to a new "bulletin" file and delete all the stage notes and texts you do not want carried fully in the bulletin. The remaining skeleton script is the bulletin.

We always use 8.5" x 11" paper unfolded and stapled like a book. This way there is no fussing about sizing and spacing to fit a folded version. It also allows a full-page cover.

Fifth, the bulletin cover is another opportunity for individual talents to shine. A youth might contribute a drawing. Someone might work up a design on a computer. A collage of newspaper headlines, spray-paint silhouettes, or sponge designs are effective. We usually make photocopies from the original.

The bulletin is a good memento for the youths' scrapbooks. Keep a stack along with copies of the script in the files for reference in later years.

WALLS

We ask that all females sit in pews to the *left* of the main aisle. Males sit to the *right*.[1]

PRELUDE

We invite you to consider the following passage while listening to the music of the Prelude.

> Violence shall no more be heard in your land, devastation or destruction within your borders; you shall call your walls Salvation, and your gates Praise (Isaiah 60:18).

WORDS OF WELCOME # WALLS[2]

Youth 1 (lectern)

> The youth of _____ Church of _____
> welcome you to this special service on Walls. Our service gathers on some of the momentous events and reaches into our biblical heritage for understanding. Our service is our hope and our gift to you.

CALL TO WORSHIP

Youth 2 (back of sanctuary)

> From Psalm 122: I was glad when they said to me, "Let us go to the house of the LORD!" Our feet are standing within your gates, O Jerusalem. . . . Pray for the peace of Jerusalem: "May they prosper who love you. Peace be within your walls, and security within your towers . . ." (1–2, 6–7).

*PROCESSIONAL HYMN[3]

"A Mighty Fortress Is Our God"
> *Martin Luther, 1529*

UNISON PRAYER

Youth 3 (lectern)

> Let us join together in reading the Unison Prayer.

Congregation

> We gather together today, young and old, men and women, boys and girls, parents and children, to ask for help and to search for understanding. We confess that although we live together, we live in a world divided. Walls of guilt and helplessness stand between those of us with homes and those of us without shelter. Walls of fear stand between those of us with AIDS and those of us who are well. Walls of competition stand between us and our peers. Walls of misunderstanding exist within our own families.

---

1. Ushers should direct people so they sit according to this plan. In addition, it is helpful to post signs.
2. This service was written the year the Berlin Wall was removed.
3. Normally the script and the bulletin include page numbers for hymns which, for obvious reason, are not listed here.

*Those who are able to stand should do so for each part of the service marked with an asterisk.

Give us, O God, the agility to scale these walls, the power to knock them down. Teach us the lessons that we may dismantle these walls brick by brick, stone by stone, and with spiritual mortar rebuild, creating places for sanctuary, rest, education, and community. We ask these things in your name, O God. Amen.

ASSURANCE

Youth 4 (lectern)

From Ephesians 2:12–14 (TEV): I say to you: "At that time you were apart from Christ. You were foreigners, and did not belong to God's chosen people. You had no part in the covenants, which were based on God's promises to his people, and you lived in this world without hope and without God. But now, in union with Christ Jesus you, who used to be far away, have been brought near by the death of Christ. For Christ himself has brought us peace by making Jews and Gentiles one people. With his own body he broke down the wall that separated them and kept them enemies."

*GLORIA PATRI

TIME WITH ADULTS

Youth 5 (standing informally with Youth 6 at the front of congregation)

In the Meditation later this hour, we will be concentrating on the stories and events involving physical walls, walls built of brick and mortar that have forcibly separated people, distanced them, put them in different camps.

Youth 6

Most of the walls of our lives, however, are not ones we can touch or see. They are, in fact, invisible. We have constructed such a wall today, here in the sanctuary. It is this aisle. And it separates for the most part the men and the women of this congregation. This aisle, today, acts as a symbol of all the invisible walls between us. It is our task and our responsibility to challenge those walls.

Youth 5

As an initial gesture of commitment that those walls will not be allowed to divide us, we would ask you now to Pass the Peace across the aisle. This is simple to do. Those people in the aisle seats will rise together, step into the aisle and shake hands with the person across the aisle from them. One will say, "The peace of Christ be with you."

Youth 6

And the other will respond, "And also with you."

Youth 5

Then people will return to their seats and, turning to the person next to them in the pew, offer the same handshake and greeting. Likewise, the greeting will be passed down each pew.

Youth 6

This is a simple symbol of shattering walls with peace. Will those on the aisle rise and extend the greeting of peace across this invisible wall.

FIRST OLD TESTAMENT RESPONSIVE READING

Youth 7 (lectern)

Join me now in reading responsively from Exodus 14:21–22.

Then Moses stretched out his hand over the sea;

Congregation

The LORD drove the sea back by a strong east wind all night, and turned the sea into dry land; and the waters were divided.

Youth 7

The Israelites went into the sea on dry ground,

Congregation

The waters forming a wall for them on their right and on their left.

SECOND OLD TESTAMENT RESPONSIVE READING

Youth 8 (lectern)

Join me in our second responsive Old Testament reading from Zechariah 2:1–5.

I looked up and saw a man with a measuring line in his hand. Then I asked, "Where are you going?"

Congregation

He answered me, "To measure Jerusalem, to see what is its width and what is its length,"

Youth 8

Then the angel who talked with me came forward, and another angel came forward to meet him, and said to him, "Run, say to that young man: Jerusalem shall be inhabited like villages without walls, because of the multitude of people and animals in it.

Congregation

For I will be a wall of fire all around it, says the LORD, and I will be the glory within it."

MEDITATION

Youth 9 (pulpit)

Our Meditation this morning is divided into three parts, one biblical and two current. We seek to understand God's witness to us and confirm that it was not just through incidents in the past but also within our own lives. We begin with the ancient story of Jericho.

Part I: God's Witness in the Past—The Wall of Jericho

The chancel table is covered with a sheet. On it is a wall made of the cardboard "bricks" popular with young children. One youth is seated under the table out of view. She holds the strings that are attached to the bricks so that she can pull on them and topple the brick walls.

All the youth not directly involved in the action sit in the choir loft (in our sanctuary on the left and right of the chancel, people facing each other across the altar table).

Youth 10 (pulpit)

From Joshua, chapter 6: As Joshua had commanded the people, the seven priests carrying the seven trumpets of rams' horns before the LORD went forward, blowing the trumpets, with the ark of the covenant of the LORD following them (v. 8).

Five pairs of youth march majestically (slowly) around the table. The first pair have swords that they carry across their chests. The second pair have trumpets. The third and fourth pair carry the ark on their shoulders. The final pair is like the first, with swords.

And the armed men went before the priests who blew the trumpets; the rear guard came after the ark, while the trumpets blew continually. To the people Joshua gave this command: "You shall not shout or let your voice be heard, nor shall you utter a word, until the day I tell you to shout. Then you shall shout." So the ark of the Lord went around the city, circling it once; and they came into the camp, and spent the night in the camp (vs. 9–11). *(Pause)*

All five pairs stop. Everyone lowers the item he or she carries (swords, trumpets, the ark). Everyone bows heads. When the reading resumes, everyone straightens up and continues "marching."

Then Joshua rose early in the morning, and the priests took up the ark of the LORD. The seven priests carrying the seven trumpets of rams' horns before the ark of the LORD passed on, blowing the trumpets continually. The armed men went before them, and the rear guard came after the ark of the Lord, while the trumpets blew continually. On the second day they marched around the city once and then returned to the camp. They did this for six days (vs. 12–14). *(Pause)*

Again, all five pairs stop, lower items, and bow heads. When the reading resumes, straighten up and continue "marching."

> On the seventh day they rose early, at dawn, and marched around the city in the same manner seven times. It was only on that day that they marched around the city seven times. And at the seventh time, when the priests had blown the trumpets, Joshua said to the people, "Shout! For the Lord has given you the city" (vs. 15–16).

All the youth in the choir loft shout!

> So the people shouted, and the trumpets were blown. As soon as the people heard the sound of the trumpets, they raised a great shout, and the wall fell down flat . . .

Youth under the the table pulls the strings!

> . . . so the people charged straight ahead into the city and captured it (v. 20).

Everyone returns to seats.

Part II: God's Witness in the Present—Rap on Race

Youth 11 (pulpit)

We now move to the present and explore the witness of our Lord in the world of today. Our second Meditation touches on an issue of both international importance and personal, daily confusion. It is our racial diversity.

Youths 12, 13, 14 present the rap. Youth come down the aisle(s) "rapping" in rhythmic, swinging step. Youth 12 says two verses; Youth 13 picks up with two more; then Youth 14. They repeat the cycle until the end.

> Now Jericho fell a long time ago,
>
> We saw God act in a wall laid low.
>
> It's a nice memory but just the same,
>
> What's it mean for the modern game?
>
> We don't live surrounded by a wall,
>
> Which we need to shout for God to make fall.
>
> But, if truth be told, we live fortified
>
> Not just by vitamins on the side.
>
> The barriers today are a different sort.
>
> Thick as brick, not measured long or short.
>
> Instead they are attitudes; fears we don't face,
>
> Of people who are different; a different race.

In daily ways, we bump against this wall.

Civil rights is moving, but slow like a crawl.

It's still noticeable when things are mixed.

Silly all that's still waiting to be fixed.

We lead our lives in a narrow way.

Better to conform than disrupt a day.

We know the routine and follow format.

Act more or less like any doormat.

But race relations are not very cool.

The facade is fixed, we know the rule.

We stay with our own, don't climb that wall.

Only when we must do we mix at all.

Now looking back, the olden days,

Some were free, others were slaves.

But that was wrong, we fought a Civil War.

Then all were free from shore to shore.

Year by year, more victories.

All could vote, without paying fees.

Schools were ruled desegregated.

Klansmen rarely congregated.

Things look better but over's not the fight,

'Til everything's equal, Black and white.

The U.S.A. has troubles very deep.

Other countries also have reason to weep.

One place in the world remained Black and white.

Whites on top, coloreds—out of sight.

A country in Africa, far south as you can go.

Where racial lines were drawn, don't you know?

Apartheid was this awful racial system.

Blacks deserved a say, whites said "resist them."

These groups lived in this stalemate.

For years no budging; did God leave them to their fate?

It's a sad, sad story of people separated.

Did God mean this when the world he created?

Whites were rich, others lived in poverty,

Separate townships, by authority.

Whites had their hospitals modern through and through.

The others had rooms to care for just a few.

Schools, buses, and restrooms were all separated.

Police used whips to keep beaches segregated.

South Africa's anguish left little to cheer.

God witnessed in the past, but left the present unclear.

For one Black leader, the years were very long.

The nights were starless, the prison walls stood strong.

It was 27 years Mandela was inside.

That's nearly ten thousand turnings of the tide.

But for all the doubts of God's work today,

The despair and death of those people far away,

There was a resurrection, they let Nelson go free!

He survived persecution, emerged for all to see!

A marvelous face, kind, honest, and true.

After 27 years it was turned to me and you.

The walls of his prison came a-tumbling down.

As mighty as the fall in Jericho town.

It gave us hope that we can be,

Released from the systems that imprison you and me.

By those prison walls God sent a vision.

Through tough times we each face a decision:

To despair and die; shattered by it all?

Or trust in God and the strength of God's call.

Walls are a way to recall this lesson.

They are always built in a sensible progression.

Yet they hurt and cut, separate and divide

Still the message of God over them can preside.

Part III: God's Witness in the Present—The Berlin Wall

Youth 11 (pulpit)

The third part of our Meditation is about another part of our world today. Europe.

Youth 15 (pulpit)

In the words of Winston Churchill in a public address at Fulton, Missouri, shortly after World War II: "Beware, I say, time may be short . . . A shadow has fallen upon the scenes so lately lighted by the Allied victory. Nobody knows what Soviet Russia and its Communist international organization intend to do in the immediate future, or what are the limits, if any, to their expansive and proselytizing tendencies . . . "

Youth 16 (lectern)

"From Stettin in the Baltic to Trieste in the Adriatic, an iron curtain has descended across the Continent. Behind that line lie all the capitals of the ancient states of central and eastern Europe."

Youth 15

Warsaw!

Youth 17 draws first curtain.[4]

Youth 16

Berlin!

Youth 18 draws next curtain.

Youth 15

Prague!

Youth 19 draws next curtain.

---

4. Our sanctuary has eight large windows with curtains. You may need to adjust this part given the design of your sanctuary.

Youth 16

Vienna!

Youth 20 draws next curtain.

Youth 15

Budapest!

Youth 21 draws next curtain.

Youth 16

Belgrade!

Youth 22 draws next curtain.

Youth 15

Bucharest!

Youth 23 draws next curtain.

Youth 16

Sofia!

Youth 24 draws next curtain.

Youth 15

From Hosea 2:6, I read to you:

> Therefore I will hedge up her way with thorns; and I will build a wall against her, so that she cannot find her paths.

Youth 16

From Habakkuk 2:11, I read to you:

> For the stones will cry out from the wall.
>
> For the stones will cry out from the wall.
>
> For the stones will cry out from the wall.

Youth 15

Since 1961 when the Berlin Wall was erected, many people tried to escape from East to West Berlin. Some tried to climb the wall. Others dug tunnels under it. Some even strapped themselves to the underside of cars so that people with authorization to cross Checkpoint Charlie could drive them out. Few reached the freedom they sought. Over eighty people were killed in these various attempts to reach the West.

Youth 16

Among those were: Michale Gartenschlager, a youth.

Youth 25 hangs a cross on the backdrop.

Youth 15

An East German schoolboy who was shot while trying to swim the Elbe on August 7, 1962.

Youth 26 hangs a cross on the backdrop.

Youth 16

An East German man also trying to swim to freedom on June 6, 1962.

Youth 25 hangs a cross on the backdrop.

Youth 15

Mr. P. Fechter.

Youth 26 hangs a cross on the backdrop.

Youth 16

An unidentified man shot on July 30, 1962.

Youth 25 hangs a cross on the backdrop.

Youth 15

An unidentified East German guard killed on October 8, 1964.

Youth 26 hangs a cross on the backdrop.

Youth 16

Dr. Karl-Heinz Nitschke.

Youth 25 hangs a cross on the backdrop.

Youth 15

We pause now for a moment of silent vigil in the memory of these seven and all the others who suffered separation, loneliness, oppression, and death in the midst of the enormous walls erected in Europe between communist and free peoples.

Wait for 30 seconds.

Youth 16

I read the following proclamation from Ezekiel 38:20, 23: [T]he fish of the sea, and the birds of the air, and the animals of the field, and all creeping things that creep on the ground, and all human beings that are on the face of the earth, shall quake at my presence, and the mountains shall be thrown down, and the cliffs shall fall, and every wall shall tumble to the ground. . . . So I will display my greatness and my holiness and make myself known in the eyes of many nations. Then they shall know that I am the LORD.

As the word Lord is said, all curtains are simultaneously drawn open. Then all youth assemble on chancel steps to sing.

SONG

"Die Gedanken sind Frei"[5]

---

5. This song can be found in numerous songbooks.

Youth 15

I quote now Vaclav Havel, Czechoslovak playwright turned president, in an address to the U.S. Congress, in February, 1990:

"When they arrested me on October 27, I was living in a country ruled by the most conservative communist government in Europe, and our society slumbered beneath the pall of a totalitarian system.

"Today, less than four months later, I'm speaking to you as the representative of a country that has set out on the road to democracy, a country where there is complete freedom of speech, which is getting ready for free elections and which wants to create a prosperous market economy and its own foreign policy.

"It is all very extraordinary . . . We are living in very extraordinary times."

CALL TO OFFERING

Youth 27

In Genesis, it is said: "Joseph is a fruitful bough, a fruitful bough by a spring, his branches run over the wall." So, too, by our generosity will the church prosper and the gospel be spread.

Youth 27 hands the offering plates to the ushers.

OFFERTORY

"May There Always Be Sunshine"[6]
                    Russian folk song

All youth gather at chancel steps to sing offertory.

May there always be sunshine (*right arm raised to the sky*)

May there always be blue sky (*left arm also raised to sky*)

May there always be parents (*both arms reach toward congregation*)

May there always be me. (*cross forearms over heart*)

Repeat two times.

*THE DOXOLOGY

*RECEIVING OF THE OFFERING

Youth 27

We offer these gifts with gratitude and hope that they may create avenues of understanding, bridges of community over the walls that divide us. Amen.

---

6. © 1964 by MCA Music Canada, a division of MCA Canada Ltd., Willowdale, Ontario. Used by permission.

PRAYERS OF THE PEOPLE

Youth 28 (lectern)

Let us bow now for prayer.

Dear God, Within the protection of your holy walls you ask us to become conscious of other walls that are not yours, false walls that divide your children from one another, walls of suspicion, walls of age, walls of gender, walls of class distinction.

Be with us here today, we pray, here, in this your sanctuary in this brief hour, where we have tried to open passageways through walls of false separation, so that we may honor this your house with all our hearts.

Be with those, also, we pray, who in this building throughout the week honor you with their work: their choir practices, their committee meetings, their struggles with alcoholism, their polishing and cleaning, their sermon writing.

Be with those who cannot enter this your house, for reasons of sickness, for reasons of fear, for reasons of passivity.

Be with all of us as we leave these walls. Help us retain a clear and pure vision of a world without barriers. Give us the courage to challenge the divisions in our families, our towns, our country. Bring us together. We ask all this in the name of our strength and our guide who taught us to pray . . .

THE LORD'S PRAYER

Congregation

Our Father, who art in heaven . . . .

* CLOSING HYMN[7]

"In Christ There Is No East or West"
Alexander Robert Reinagle, 1836

* BENEDICTION

Youth (gathered at the chancel steps)

And now shall we go forth to the East and to the West, in peace, united by the graciousness of our God.

Congregation

Together may we share the light of God's countenance upon us. May God bless you, children, and keep you.

Youth

And may God bless you, too, O Children of God.

POSTLUDE

---

7. This hymn is implicitly rather than explicitly about walls. We chose it for its connection with the Berlin story in the Meditation as well as the verse about children which fits well.

The following is a list and description of the things needed in the service. We have organized them by the order required.

The Backdrop

We built a backdrop for this service. It has been carefully stored over the years so that we can paint it and use it again. The basic structure is four panels hinged together and built with triangular braces at the back. It is eight feet high and almost nine feet wide. The frame is basic two-by-fours. The screen is stretched, heavy canvas. It was built as if it were a stage-set backdrop.

WALLS

For this service, we painted large, gray boulders to look like a stone wall. The ones at the bottom were slightly larger than those at the top, which made it visually more solid and realistic.

The backdrop has been well worth the effort and resources it took to make it. The effect it creates for those entering the sanctuary is an immediate sense that something is special about the service. However, it is very simple and does not create the feeling of theater. It fits at the front of our sanctuary between the lectern and the pulpit. When we use it the youth do not sit in the choir stalls, but instead claim the first rows of pews in the congregation.

For the Walls service we used the backdrop as a place to hang the memorial crosses during the Meditation for those who died trying to cross the Berlin Wall. To prepare for this we inserted hefty straight pins into the canvas before the service.

Signs at the Entrance

In this service we created an artificial wall by asking the females to sit on one side of the congregation while the males sat on the other side. Although this was explained in the bulletin and the ushers were carefully giving directions, it was helpful to have directional signs with big arrows pointing out the appropriate side for seating.

Meditation on Jericho

The Wall

You will need a large white sheet, cardboard "fake brick" children's blocks, string, and pins. Cover a table at the front of the sanctuary with the sheet so the congregation cannot see what is under the table. Stack the blocks to look like a walled city. Attach the string with the pins to various foundation blocks. A youth sits under the table with the ends of the strings. When the wall is to "fall" he or she simply pulls on the string.

Cardboard Swords

Make four large cardboard swords. Cover the "blade" with aluminum foil to give it a shine. Each "soldier" can fashion his or her sword handle and decorate it.

Cardboard Trumpets

Using cardboard, cut out two large curling "ram's horns." Paint them white (or another strong color that is not brown) so they stand out.

The Ark

Have some fun making the ark. At minimum it can be a box on top of two parallel broom sticks spray painted gold. You can add a roof. To make it look carved, cover the box with shapes made from whipped soap flakes and water, which, when dried, can be painted.

Costumes

These can be simple robes tied at the waist with rope or strips of colorful cloth. Headdresses add to the pageantry of the story.

Meditation on Race (the Rap)

The youth that performed the rap insisted on costumes. They wore baggy loud pants, T-shirts, sunglasses, and baseball caps (backwards). They changed into these clothes just for the rap.

Meditation on Berlin

We needed seven white, heavy paper crosses to hang on the pins stuck into the painted canvas wall. The crosses were made of heavy paper but not cardboard, which would have been too heavy. They were a foot tall but could have been bigger. We left them plain. Had we made bigger ones we would have considered writing on them the names of the victims or the dates of their deaths. The smaller crosses needed to be simple.

WALLS

BULLETIN

We ask that all females sit in pews to the *left* of the main aisle. Males sit to the *right*.

PRELUDE

We invite you to consider the following passage while listening to the music of the Prelude. Reading from Isaiah 60:18:

> Violence shall no more be heard in your land,
> devastation or destruction within your borders;
> you shall call your walls Salvation, and your gates Praise.

WORDS OF WELCOME

CALL TO WORSHIP

*PROCESSIONAL HYMN

"A Mighty Fortress Is Our God"
> *Martin Luther, 1529*

UNISON PRAYER

Congregation

> We gather together today, young and old, men and women, boys and girls, parents and children, to ask for help and to search for understanding. We confess that although we live together, we live in a world divided. Walls of guilt and helplessness stand between those of us with homes and those of us without shelter. Walls of fear stand between those of us with AIDS and those of us who are well. Walls of competition stand between us and our peers. Walls of misunderstanding exist within our own families.

> Give us, O God, the agility to scale these walls, the power to knock them down. Teach us the lessons that we may dismantle these walls brick by brick, stone by stone, and with spiritual mortar rebuild, creating places for sanctuary, rest, education, and community. We ask these things in your name, O God. Amen.

ASSURANCE

*GLORIA PATRI

TIME WITH ADULTS

FIRST OLD TESTAMENT RESPONSIVE READING

Exodus 14:21–22

Leader

> Then Moses stretched out his hand over the sea;

Congregation

The LORD drove the sea back by a strong east wind all night, and turned the sea into dry land; and the waters were divided.

Leader

The Israelites went into the sea on dry ground,

Congregation

the waters forming a wall for them on their right and on their left.

SECOND OLD TESTAMENT RESPONSIVE READING

Zechariah 2:1–5

Leader

I looked up and saw a man with a measuring line in his hand. Then I asked, "Where are you going?"

Congregation

He answered me, "To measure Jerusalem, to see what is its width and what is its length."

Leader

Then, the angel who talked with me came forward, and another angel came forward to meet him, and said to him, "Run, say to that young man: Jerusalem shall be inhabited like villages without walls, because of the multitude of people and animals in it.

Congregation

"For I will be to her a wall of fire all around it, says the LORD, and I will be the glory within it."

MEDITATION

Part I: God's Witness in the Past—The Wall of Jericho

Part II: God's Witness in the Present—Rap on Race

Now Jericho fell a long time ago,

We saw God act in a wall laid low.

It's a nice memory but just the same,

What's it mean for the modern game?

We don't live surrounded by a wall,

Which we need to shout for God to make fall.

But, if truth be told, we live fortified

Not just by vitamins on the side.

The barriers today are a different sort.

Thick as brick, not measured long or short.

Instead they are attitudes; fears we don't face,

Of people who are different; a different race.

In daily ways, we bump against this wall.

Civil rights is moving, but slow like a crawl.

It's still noticeable when things are mixed.

Silly all that's still waiting to be fixed.

We lead our lives in a narrow way.

Better to conform than disrupt a day.

We know the routine and follow format.

Act more or less like any doormat.

But race relations are not very cool.

The facade is fixed, we know the rule.

We stay with our own, don't climb that wall.

Only when we must do we mix at all.

Now looking back, the olden days,

Some were free, others were slaves.

But that was wrong, we fought a Civil War.

Then all were free from shore to shore.

Year by year, more victories.

All could vote, without paying fees.

Schools were ruled desegregated.

Klansmen rarely congregated.

Things look better but over's not the fight,

'Til everything's equal, Black and white.

The U.S.A. has troubles very deep.

Other countries also have reason to weep.

One place in the world remained Black and white.

Whites on top, coloreds—out of sight.

A country in Africa, far south as you can go.

Where racial lines were drawn, don't you know.

Apartheid was this awful racial system.

Blacks deserved a say, whites said "resist them."

These groups lived in this stalemate.

For years no budging; did God leave them to their fate?

It's a sad, sad story of people separated.

Did God mean this when the world he created?

Whites were rich, others lived in poverty,

Separate townships, by authority.

Whites had their hospitals modern through and through.

The others had rooms to care for just a few.

Schools, buses and restrooms were all separated.

Police used whips to keep beaches segregated.

South Africa's anguish left little to cheer.

God witnessed in the past, but left the present unclear.

For one Black leader, the years were very long.

The nights were starless, the prison walls stood strong.

It was 27 years Mandela was inside.

That's nearly ten thousand turnings of the tide.

But for all the doubts of God's work today,

The despair and death of those people far away,

There was a resurrection, they let Nelson go free!

He survived persecution, emerged for all to see!

A marvelous face, kind, honest, and true.

After 27 years it was turned to me and you.

The walls of his prison came a-tumbling down.

As mighty as the fall in Jericho town.

It gave us hope that we can be,

Released from the systems that imprison you and me.

By those prison walls God sent a vision.

Through tough times we each face a decision:

To despair and die; shattered by it all?

Or trust in God and the strength of God's call.

Walls are a way to recall this lesson.

They are always built in a sensible progression.

Yet they hurt and cut, separate and divide

Still the message of God over them can preside.

Part III: God's Witness in the Present—The Berlin Wall

SONG

"Die Gedanken sind Frei"
Traditional

CALL TO OFFERING

OFFERTORY

"May There Always Be Sunshine"
Russian folk song

*THE DOXOLOGY

*RECEIVING OF THE OFFERING

PRAYERS OF THE PEOPLE

THE LORD'S PRAYER

*CLOSING HYMN

"In Christ There Is No East Or West"
Alexander Robert Reinagle, 1836

* BENEDICTION

Youth

And now shall we go forth to the East and to the West, in peace, united by the graciousness of our God.

Congregation

Together may we share the light of God's countenance upon us. May God bless you, children, and keep you.

Youth

And may God bless you, too, O Children of God.

POSTLUDE

*Those who are able, please stand.

WATER

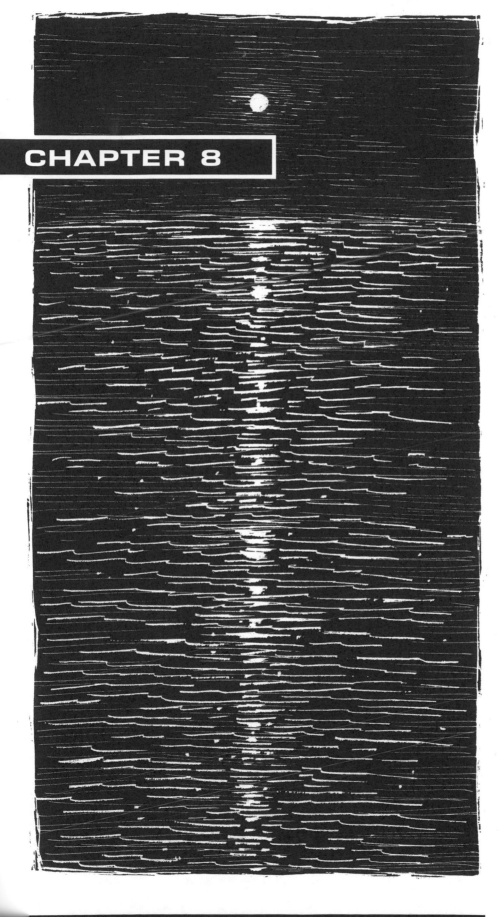

CHAPTER 8

PRELUDE

We invite you to consider the following passage while listening to the music of the Prelude. Reading from John 7:37–38:

> On the last day of the festival, the great day, while Jesus was standing there, he cried out, "Let anyone who is thirsty come to me, and let the one who believes in me drink. As the scripture has said, 'Out of the believer's heart shall flow rivers of living water.' "

WATER[1]

WORDS OF WELCOME

Youth 1 (lectern)

The youth of _____ Church of _____ welcome you to this special service which we, the young people, plan and lead.

Youth 2 (pulpit)

Many of us have spent much of the last year watching and listening to messages from the desert. In response, we chose the theme of water for our service. As a gift of life, water has special meaning to us this spring. As we explore it we reach both into our current lives and into our biblical heritage for understanding. Our service is our hope and our gift to you.

CALL TO WORSHIP

Youth 3 (back of sanctuary)

Reading from John 4:6–15: . . . Jesus, tired out by his journey, was sitting by the well. It was about noon. A Samaritan woman came to draw water, and Jesus said to her, . . . "Every one who drinks of this water will be thirsty again, but those who drink of the water that I will give them will never be thirsty. The water that I will give will become in them a spring of water gushing up to eternal life." The woman said to him, "Sir, give me this water, so that I may never be thirsty or have to keep coming here to draw water."

* PROCESSIONAL HYMN

"Guide Me, O Thou Great Jehovah"
John Hughes, 1907

UNISON PRAYER OF CONFESSION

Youth 4 (lectern)

Let us join together in reading the Unison Prayer of Confession as printed in the bulletin.

---

1. This service was written in 1991, the year of the Persian Gulf War.

*Those who are able to stand should do so for each part of the service marked with an asterisk.

We gather here together today to confess our estrangement from each other and from you. We acknowledge that we have turned our backs on those in need around us. Too often we have allowed ourselves to be swayed by the glitter and the riches of the world only to realize we have been torn from you, our Strength and our Guide. We remember the people of Israel, pulled from their homes, in exile in Babylon. They wept for their land and their temple. They longed for the things they remembered. We, too, confess our mistakes and mourn our loss. We long to find again the loving relationship with our Lord. We ask you to hear us. These our prayers to you. Amen.

INTERPRETIVE DANCE[2]

"By the Waters of Babylon"
>   *Jewish melody*

By the waters, the waters of Babylon,

We sat down and wept,

And wept for Zion.

We remember,

we remember,

we remember Zion.

The dance includes five girls dressed in black leotards and soft-colored wraparound skirts. (Our service used girls as the dancers. There's no reason, however, that boys can't be dancers as well.) Their movements are very simple; each musical line has a gesture that is formed and held like a tableau.

"By the waters . . ."

Each girl walks in holding a "harp" and forms a row, angling away from congregation as if by a riverside. When each "reaches the bank" she acts as if she dips her hand in the water and watches it drip back down into the river.

"We sat down . . ."

Together the ones in the back kneel to give some height dimension to the tableau, and the others sit. They bend over their heads so their hair (brushed loosely, not tied back) falls over their faces. In the process each lays her harp on the floor.

"When we remember Zion . . ."

---

2. We inserted a dance into the Prayer of Confession. This service was held during the time that the Kurds were in mass flight inside of Iraq. Although there is no direct mention of this news in the service, this dance evoked that plight. The congregation did not miss the allusion and many later commented that this part of the service was particularly moving and spiritual for them.

Each girls shifts up a level (sitting ones to kneeling; kneeling ones to standing) and holds one hand palm up about head level and shifts gaze upward.

"There we hang our harps . . . "

Each girl gracefully stoops to pick up her harp and in a slow line files by the backdrop and hangs the harp on the pins provided. The harps are left there for the rest of the service.

ASSURANCE OF PARDON

Youth 5 (lectern)

From the prophet Ezekiel we read, Thus says the Lord GOD . . . "I will sprinkle clean water upon you, and you shall be clean from all your uncleanesses, and from all your idols I will cleanse you" (Ezekiel 36:25). Believe what God has said.

*GLORIA PATRI

TIME WITH ADULTS: A WAVE

Youth line up across the front of the sanctuary facing the congregation.

Youth 6

This is the part of the service we usually call "Time with Children." It is a time when the children come forward and a simple version of the day's message is explained to them. Today, we are going to hold to that tradition. We will attempt to experience in a simple way the core message of today's service. We want to feel the power, the unity, and the strength of water in our Christian faith. We want to enact that strong, unified, surging quality. To do that, we as a whole room full of people are going to make a wave.

First, let me explain as simply as possible how this is to be done.

Any of you who have been to a major sports event or watched the Olympics on television understand the concept of a wave. Each of you should have received a piece of colored construction paper when you entered the church today. You should now take that in your hands and put down anything else you might be holding—like a hymnbook or a bulletin.

The youth will lead the wave from the front of the sanctuary. Together we will raise our colored papers high up in the air and then lower them. As this is done, those people on the right side of the congregation—that is your right facing the front, the lectern side—will create the first wave. They do this row by row, beginning at the front. Each row in turn will stand up and hold their paper high up in the air and then sit down. This should be done in a single and smooth motion—stand, raise your arms, and then sit down. Don't rush it and make it jumpy.

The youth will watch until the last row on the right side completes the wave. Then they will initiate a second wave down the left side of the sanctuary.

When the second "wave" reaches the back of the left side, the youth will initiate a third and last wave. This wave will be for the whole congregation—front to back.

So, to review, there are three waves in all. First the right side, then the left side, and finally the whole congregation. The youth will be the leaders for all three.

And now, if you are all set, we will begin.

OLD TESTAMENT READING

Youth 7 (lectern)

The Old Testament Reading for today is Exodus 14:15–18, 21–25.

Then the LORD said to Moses, "Why do you cry out to me? Tell the Israelites to go forward. But you lift up your staff, and stretch out your hand over the sea and divide it, that the Israelites may go into the sea on dry ground. Then I will harden the hearts of the Egyptians so that they will go in after them; and so I will gain glory for myself over Pharaoh and all his army, his chariots, and his chariot drivers. And the Egyptians shall know that I am the LORD . . ."

Then Moses stretched out his hand over the sea. The LORD drove the sea back by a strong east wind all night, and turned the sea into dry land; and the waters were divided. The Israelites went into the sea on dry ground, the waters forming a wall for them on their right and on their left. The Egyptians pursued, and went into the sea after them, all of Pharaoh's horses, chariots, and chariot drivers. At the morning watch the LORD in the pillar of fire and cloud looked down upon the Egyptian army, and threw the Egyptian army into panic. He clogged their chariot wheels so that they turned with great difficulty. The Egyptians said, " . . . the LORD is fighting for the Israelites against us. Let's get out of here!"

ANTHEM

"Wade in the Water"
> *Traditional*

NEW TESTAMENT READING

Youth 8 (lectern)

The New Testament reading for today comes from Mark 4:37–41.

A great windstorm arose, and the waves beat into the boat, so that the boat was already being swamped. But he was in the stern, asleep on the cushion; and they woke him and said to him, "Teacher, do you not care that we are perishing?" He woke up and rebuked the wind, and said to the sea, "Peace!

Be still!" Then the wind ceased, and there was a dead calm. He said to them, "Why are you afraid? Have you still no faith?" And they were filled with great awe and said to one another, "Who then is this, that even the wind and the sea obey him?"

MEDITATION

Youth 9 (pulpit)

Our Meditation this morning is divided into four parts. We seek to understand God's witness to us and confirm that it was not just through incidents in the past but also within our own lives that God's word can be made known to us.

Part I: Water as a Destructive Force

Youths 10 and 11 present the rap. They follow each other down the main aisle "rapping" in rhythmic, swinging step. They alternate verses.

For forty nights and forty days,

Yahweh was on a rainy craze.

The water fell and drummed and beat,

On village roof and city street.

The people watched as water rose,

It crept along wherever it chose.

The streams began to run together,

The world was in for some heavy weather.

They watched the water come under doors,

Forming pools on the floors.

And soon there was no floor to see,

As it got deep—one foot, two, three.

They climbed the stairs and began to cry,

There was no way in which to dry.

The floods did not slow down nor stop,

And slowly did they reach the top.

The people climbed out on the roofs,

The air was filled with screams of proof,

They were all frightened, sinking fast.

The world was caving in at last.

It was clear that God was mad.

God saw the world had gone bad,

And used the water to make the point,

It was to kill—not to anoint.

God sent to earth the pounding rain,

The sound alone could numb the brain.

But worse than that, it wouldn't stop,

And lakes climbed to the mountaintop.

God wiped out everything on the earth,

Except for some on Noah's berth.

God was never acting coy,

The water sent was to destroy.

As time has passed, its turned a new leaf,

Water can still stand for grief.

We all know stories of flood and hail,

Of loss of navies as they sail.

We fear the floods, of falling in,

Of being lost in dark and din.

We think of being pulled way down,

And what it must be like to drown.

Bad water can bring bad disease,

Or drought can kill off crops and trees.

Swampy water has mosquitoes,

Undammed water too quickly flows.

Acid rain is now a fear,

It brings harms, its costs are dear.

Love Canal was poisonous,

The water there was cancerous.

We fear the lead that lines the pipes,

And chemicals of different types,

That into our water creep.

To clean it up is not too cheap.

While water is an act of nature,

It also has another feature.

Water can be an evil tool,

When one wants over another to rule.

Water torture is very horrid,

And other ways are also sordid.

Once fire hoses symbolized

How demonstrators were pacified.

To us as Christians water seems

To bring forth life and fruitful themes.

But the darker side is often there:

Water also brings God's words: Beware.

We've seen the lessons water brings,

To those who turn their backs on things,

Who think humans, not God, wear the crown,

And in the flood found their error drowned.

Part II: Water in Trouble

Youth 12 reads the Bible verses from the pulpit. The other three youth read from various corners of the sanctuary and balcony.

Youth 12 (pulpit)

We will now turn to the second part of the Meditation, Water in Trouble. Reading from Psalm 65:9–10:

You visit the earth and water it, you greatly enrich it; the river of God is full of water; you provide the people with grain, for so you have prepared it. You water its furrows abundantly, settling its ridges, softening it with showers, and blessing its growth.

Youth 13

In some countries only a third of the people have safe, clean water.

Youth 12

Job 22:7. You have given no water to the weary to drink, and you have withheld bread from the hungry.

Youth 14

When the people of Colorado Springs shovel their snow, they carefully shovel it onto their lawns. The annual rainfall is so low, every little bit of moisture on the gardens is treasured. Are we all this careful?

Youth 12

Jeremiah 15:18. Why is my pain unceasing, my wound incurable, refusing to be healed? Truly, you are to me like a deceitful brook, like waters that fail.

Youth 15

Dysentery, caused primarily by a lack of safe water, kills six million children every year, and contributes to the death of 18 million people.

Youth 12

Isaiah 21:14. Bring water to the thirsty, meet the fugitive with bread.

Youth 13

People who must carry water from a well or river use only about three gallons a day. We use twice that much whenever we flush the toilet.

Youth 12

Isaiah 41:17. When the poor and needy seek water, and there is none, and their tongue is arched with thirst, I the LORD will answer them.

Youth 14

The World Health Organization estimates that 80 percent of all disease worldwide is caused by inadequate water or sanitation.

Youth 12

Psalm 107:35. [God] turns a desert into pools of water, a parched land into springs of water.

Youth 15

Most of the rural women of the world must do all their washing in a river or stream.

Youth 12

Amos 5:24. But let justice roll down like waters, and righteousness like an ever flowing stream.

Youths 13, 14, and 15 in unison

What is the longest that you have had to suffer from thirst?

Part III: Water as a Nurturing Force

Youth 16 (pulpit)

For the third part of the Meditation we present an anthem.

ANTHEM

"Lord, You Have Come to the Lakeshore"[3]

Cesáreo Gabaráin

This song is sung partly in Spanish. The congregation is invited to follow along in the hymnal.

Part IV: Water as a Redemptive Force

Youth 16 (pulpit)

We now move to the fourth and final part of the Meditation, Water as a Redemptive Force. As Christians we celebrate the Sacrament of Baptism when water is used as a symbol of a new life.

The youth congregate at the front of the sanctuary in a line. Each has a baptism sign. On it in large and clear letters is the date of that youth's baptism. Each one in turn steps forward and says: "I was baptized on . . . in (city, state)."

Youth 16

In recognition that baptism marks the beginning of the journey of faith for all believers, please stand if you are able and join me in the unison reading of the baptism affirmation found in your bulletin.

*BAPTISM AFFIRMATION

Congregation

We believe that in baptism

the Spirit demonstrates and confirms God's promise

to include us and our children in this gracious covenant,

cleansing us from sin,

and giving us newness of life,

as participants in Christ's death and resurrection.

Baptism sets us in the visible community of Christ's people

and joins us to all other believers by a powerful bond.

In baptism we give ourselves up in faith and repentance to be the Lord's.

---

3. We used a hymn for the anthem and sang it in both Spanish and English.

For both children and adults, baptism is a reminder that God loves us long before we can love God.

* HYMN

"Baptized in Water"
Gaelic melody

CALL TO OFFERING

Youth 17

Isaiah 21:14 reads: Bring water to the thirsty, meet the fugitive with bread.

OFFERTORY

"Fill My Cup"
Isaiah Jones, Jr., 1969

* THE DOXOLOGY

* RECEIVING OF THE OFFERING

Youth 17

And the one who was seated on the throne said, . . . "It is done! I am the Alpha and the Omega, the beginning and the end. To the thirsty I will give water as a gift from the spring of the water of life" (Revelation 21:5, 6).

So, too, do we give of our lives unto the work of the Lord. Amen.

PRAYERS OF THE PEOPLE

Youth 18

Let us bow now for prayer:

Dear God, Creator of this world in all its natural beauty, we thank you for the lakes that are like mirrors, the flowing streams, the foamy pounding surf, and the morning dew. We thank you for the sprinkling rain on our faces, the puddles that invite a good stomp from our boots, the cold water rushing out of the hose and all over our chins, and the warm bath at night before we go to bed. We see life in the water around us, and we are in awe of your power. And yet we also remember how fragile water can be, and we ask for your help and strength as we renew our efforts to provide clean and safe water to all your people.

Dear God, Redeemer, we thank you for the symbol of water in our lives, the rituals of water in our worship. In baptism we are anointed by water and blessed with new life. With each new baptism we can again renew our promises with you.

Dear God, Parent to us all, we thank you for the love and joy that surround the youth of this church. As we celebrate Youth Sunday, we can all remember the spontaneity and the wonder we all feel as children of God. We give thanks for life and for those who nurture and care for the young people of this congregation. We are grateful for the witness of your love made known as generation succeeds generation.

And finally, dear God, help us to find true peace. Remind us constantly that in water there is life, in your reign there is peace.

We ask all this in the name of our strength and our guide who taught us to pray . . .

THE LORD'S PRAYER

Congregation

Our Father, who art in heaven . . . .

* CLOSING HYMN

"I've Got Peace Like a River"
African-American spiritual

* BENEDICTION

Youth (gathered at the chancel steps)

And now shall we go forth into the world, in peace, surrounded by the wonders of ocean and land, united by the graciousness of our God.

Congregation

Together may we share the light of God's countenance upon us. May God bless you children, and keep you.

Youth

And may the Lord bless you, too, O Children of God.

POSTLUDE

PROPS AND PARAPHERNALIA

The following is a list and description of the things needed in the service. We have organized them by the order required.

Bulletin Insert

Each person was given an 8.5" x 11" sheet of green, blue, or silver construction paper with their bulletin. These colored sheets were for the congregational wave which is part of "Time with Adults."

The Backdrop

We recycled the backdrop from the Walls service. We painted it with a scene of a stream and weeping-willow branches trailing in the water. This scene is largely meant as a backdrop for the Interpretive Dance. We stuck pairs of large straight pins into the canvas for the dancers to use when hanging their harps.

Interpretive Dance

The dancers wore black leotards, black tights, and soft colored knee-length wrap-around skirts. Each carried a lightweight hand harp. We made the harps each about 18 inches high, cutting the frame out of white poster board. We taped rows of white strings (for visibility) to look as if the harps could be strummed.

Meditation: Part I—Water as a Destructive Force (the Rap)

The two youth dressed for the rap by wearing baggy shorts, loud shirts, sunglasses, and baseball caps (backwards).

Meditation: Part IV—Water as a Redemptive Force

We gave each youth a large sheet of white poster board cut in the shape of a water drop. With felt-tipped markers they each wrote the date and place of his or her baptism.

WATER

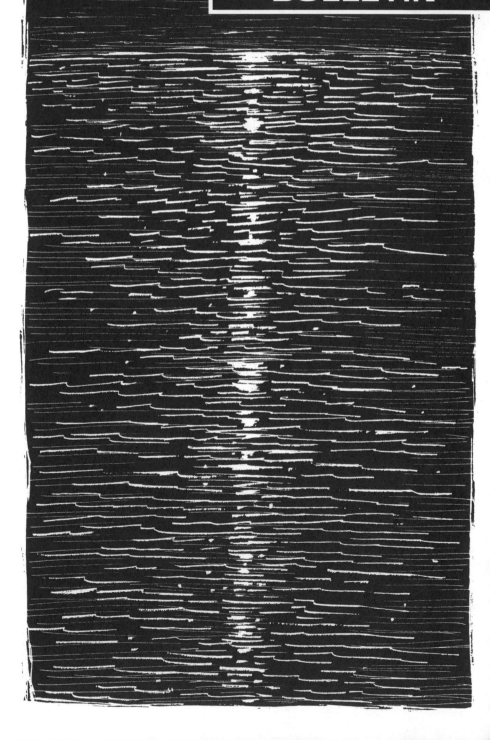

PRELUDE

We invite you to consider the following passage while listening to the music of the Prelude.

> On the last day of the festival, the great day, while Jesus was standing there, he cried out, "Let anyone who is thirsty come to me, and let the one who believes in me drink. As the scripture has said, 'Out of the believer's heart shall flow rivers of living water'" (John 7:37–38).

WORDS OF WELCOME

CALL TO WORSHIP

*PROCESSIONAL HYMN

"Guide Me, O Thou Great Jehovah"
John Hughes, 1907

UNISON PRAYER OF CONFESSION

Congregation

> We gather here together today to confess our estrangement from each other and from you. We acknowledge that we have turned our backs on those in need around us. Too often we have allowed ourselves to be swayed by the glitter and the riches of the world only to realize we have been torn from you, our Strength and our Guide. We remember the people of Israel, pulled from their homes, in exile in Babylon. They wept for their land and their temple. They longed for the things they remembered. We, too, confess our mistakes and mourn our loss. We long to find again the loving relationship with our Creator. We ask you to hear us. These our prayers to you. Amen.

INTERPRETIVE DANCE

"By the Waters of Babylon"
Jewish melody

ASSURANCE OF PARDON

*GLORIA PATRI

TIME WITH ADULTS: A WAVE

OLD TESTAMENT READING

Exodus 14:15–18, 21–25

ANTHEM

"Wade in the Water"
Traditional

NEW TESTAMENT READING

Mark 4:37–41

MEDITATION

Part I: Water as a Destructive Force

For forty nights and forty days,

Yahweh was on a rainy craze.

The water fell and drummed and beat,

On village roof and city street.

The people watched as water rose,

It crept along wherever it chose.

The streams began to run together,

The world was in for some heavy weather.

They watched the water come under doors,

Forming pools on the floors.

And soon there was no floor to see,

As it got deep—one foot, two, three.

They climbed the stairs and began to cry,

There was no way in which to dry.

The floods did not slow down nor stop,

And slowly did they reach the top.

The people climbed out on the roofs,

The air was filled with screams of proof,

They were all frightened, sinking fast.

The world was caving in at last.

It was clear that God was mad.

God saw the world had gone bad,

And used the water to make the point,

It was to kill—not to anoint.

God sent to earth the pounding rain,

The sound alone could numb the brain.

But worse than that, it wouldn't stop,

And lakes climbed to the mountaintop.

He wiped out everything on the earth,

Except for some on Noah's berth.

God was never acting coy,

The water sent was to destroy.

As time has passed, its turned a new leaf,

Water can still stand for grief.

We all know stories of flood and hail,

Of loss of navies as they sail.

We fear the floods, of falling in,

Of being lost in dark and din.

We think of being pulled way down,

And what it must be like to drown.

Bad water can bring bad disease,

Or drought can kill off crops and trees.

Swampy water has mosquitoes,

Undammed water too quickly flows.

Acid rain is now a fear,

It brings harms, its costs are dear.

Love Canal was poisonous,

The water there was cancerous.

We fear the lead that lines the pipes,

And chemicals of different types,

That into our water creep.

To clean it up is not too cheap.

While water is an act of nature,

It also has another feature.

Water can be an evil tool,

When one wants over another to rule.

Water torture is very horrid,

And other ways are also sordid.

Once fire hoses symbolized

How demonstrators were pacified.

To us as Christians water seems

To bring forth life and fruitful themes.

But the darker side is often there:

Water also brings God's words: Beware.

We've seen the lessons water brings,

To those who turn their backs on things,

Who think humans, not God, wear the crown,

And in the flood found their error drowned.

Part II: Water in Trouble

Part III: Water as a Nurturing Force

ANTHEM

"Lord, You Have Come to the Lakeshore"
                    Cesáreo Gabaráin

This song is sung partly in Spanish. The congregation is invited to follow along in the hymnal.

Part IV: Water as a Redemptive Force

*BAPTISM AFFIRMATION

Congregation
   We believe that in baptism

      the Spirit demonstrates and confirms God's promise

      to include us and our children in this gracious covenant,

         cleansing us from sin,

and giving us newness of life,

as participants in Christ's death and resurrection.

Baptism sets us in the visible community of Christ's people

and joins us to all other believers by a powerful bond.

In baptism we give ourselves up in faith and repentance to be the Lord's.

For both children and adults, baptism is a reminder that God loves us long before we can love God.

* HYMN

"Baptized in Water"
Gaelic melody

CALL TO OFFERING

OFFERTORY

"Fill My Cup"
Isaiah Jones, Jr., 1969

* THE DOXOLOGY

* RECEIVING OF THE OFFERING

PRAYERS OF THE PEOPLE

THE LORD'S PRAYER

* CLOSING HYMN

"I've Got Peace Like a River"
African-American spiritual

* BENEDICTION

Youth
And now shall we go forth into the world, in peace, surrounded by the wonders of ocean and land, united by the graciousness of our God.

Congregation
Together may we share the light of God's countenance upon us. May God bless you children, and keep you.

Youth
And may God bless you, too, O Children of God.

POSTLUDE

*Those who are able, please stand.

FEET

CHAPTER 9

SCRIPT

Please remove your shoes before entering the Sanctuary.

PRELUDE

We invite you to consider the following passage while listening to the music of the Prelude. The Reading is from Psalm 99, verse 5:

> Extol the LORD our God;
>> worship at God's footstool!
>> Holy is God!

FEET

WORDS OF WELCOME

Youth 1 (pulpit)

The youth of _____ Church of _____ welcome you to this special service that the young people of the church plan and lead. Our theme for today is *feet*. Feet are a symbol, a somewhat unexpected, at times aching, often dancing, bottom-up or ground-up symbol of the journey we are on together as Christians. As the youth of the congregation, we can identify with those traits: We represent the unexpected; at times we ache, we often dance, and we are an emerging, bottom-up or ground-up group of people within the church. For all this we are grateful and we invite you to join in the celebration, as we take our hats off . . . to feet.

CHORAL INTROIT

"Alleluia, Alleluia! Give Thanks!"
> *Donald Fishel, 1973*

Alleluia, alleluia, we walk in the path of God

Alleluia, alleluia, we follow God's way.[1]

UNISON CALL TO WORSHIP

Youth 2 (back of sanctuary)

Let us join together in reading the words of the Unison Call to Worship

Congregation

Suddenly Jesus met them and said, "Greetings!" And they came to him, took hold of his feet, and worshiped him (Matt. 28:9).

---

1. The words are ones we wrote to match this tune.

*PROCESSIONAL HYMN

"Praise, My Soul, the King of Heaven"

John Goss, 1869

*UNISON PRAYER OF ADORATION AND THANKSGIVING

Youth 3 (lectern)

Let us join together reading the Unison Prayer of Adoration and Thanksgiving as printed in the bulletin.

Congregation

We have come together today, O God, joined in the pathway of life that you have provided. We rejoice that in Jesus we have been taught to walk this path in peace, love, and harmony. We offer thanks that the challenges of this path, its twists, turns, and distance, are not for us to travel alone. You are our guide. You are our vista. You are our resting point. We are privileged to continue our journey with you, and in our hearts we are grateful. Amen.

ANTHEM

"I've Got a Robe"

Traditional

WORDS OF ASSURANCE

Youth 4 (lectern)

From the book of Ephesians we know these words: For once you were darkness, but now in the Lord you are light. Live as children of light (5:8).

Believe what God has said and follow in God's way.

*GLORIA PATRI

TIME WITH ADULTS

"Make a Joyful Noise (with Our Feet)"

Youth 5 (at front of congregation)

For Time with Adults today, we are going to use our feet to make a joyful noise unto the Lord. This will be easy to do but only if we are all clear on the directions. Otherwise, our joyful noise will sound more like a stampede.

To put it simply, we want everyone to remain seated and stamp to a rhythm that we will teach you. The rhythm is simple. It is like this: (clap and count 1–2–3–4; 1–2–3–4)

The youth are now going to demonstrate it for you both clapping and stamping with their feet. *(Piano joins the stamping)*[2]

---

2. The organist moved to the piano and beat out the rhythm using chords in the bass clef like drums supporting the stamping.

*Those who are able to stand should do so for each part of the service marked with an asterisk.

We would like you to do it now with your feet, just once, when we signal. Here we go. *(Youth stomp and clap.)* Okay, that was half stampede and half joyful noise. Let's practice once more. Here we go. *(Stomp and clap.)*

Now we will do it for real. We will repeat the rhythm four times. The piano will be playing with us. We also invite you to clap to the rhythm.

Here we go.

OLD TESTAMENT READING

While the following passage is read, four youth enact the scene that the reading describes. Three girls dress in dark leotards and black skirts. Each has two bright fire-colored scarves. The fourth is a boy dressed as Moses with a headdress, a staff, and, most important, sandals.

Youth 6 (lectern)

The Old Testament Reading for today is Exodus 3:1–6:

Moses enters on the right, and leans on his staff.

Moses was keeping the flock of his father-in-law Jethro, the priest of Midian; he led his flock beyond the wilderness, and came to Horeb, the mountain of God.

Three girls enter, form a tight circle with backs to each other so they face outward. Begin to wave their scarves up and down like flames. Do not stop until the reading is over.

There the angel of the LORD appeared to him in a flame of fire out of a bush; he looked, and the bush was blazing, yet it was not consumed.

Moses moves two steps toward the "bush." Then abruptly turns, facing away from the congregation.

Then Moses said, "I must turn aside and see this great sight, and why the bush is not burned up." When the LORD saw that he had turned aside to see, God called to him out of the bush, "Moses, Moses!"

Moses turns toward the "bush."

And he said, "Here am I." Then he said, "Come no closer! Remove the sandals from your feet, for the place on which you are standing is holy ground."

Moses bends over, removes sandals, then straightens up.

He said further, "I am the God of your father, the God of Abraham, the God of Isaac, and the God of Jacob."

Moses turns away from "bush" and covers face with arm.

And Moses hid his face, for he was afraid to look at God.

FIRST NEW TESTAMENT READING

Youth 7 (lectern)

The first New Testament Reading for today is Mark 1:12–13.

And the Spirit immediately drove him out into the wilderness. He was in the wilderness forty days, tempted by Satan; and he was with the wild beasts; and the angels waited on him.

* HYMN

"Jesus Walked This Lonesome Valley"
American spiritual

SECOND NEW TESTAMENT READING[3]

Youth 8 (lectern)

The second New Testament Reading for today is Matthew 10:5–6, 9–14.

These twelve Jesus sent out with the following instructions: "Go nowhere among the Gentiles, and enter no town of the Samaritans, but go rather to the lost sheep of the house of Israel. . . . Take no gold, or silver, or copper in your belts, no bag for your journey, or two tunics, or sandals, or a staff; for laborers deserve their food. Whatever town or village you enter, find out who in it is worthy, and stay there until you leave. As you enter the house, greet it. If the house is worthy, let your peace come upon it; but if it is not worthy, let your peace return to you. If anyone will not welcome you or listen to your words, shake off the dust from your feet as you leave that house or town."

ANTHEM

"Guide My Feet"[4]
African-American spiritual

MEDITATIONS

Part I: Shoes and the Bible

Youth 9 (pulpit)

We will now begin the Meditation with a brief look at shoes and the Bible. We will be sharing with you an instructional lesson on how feet walked through the Bible, so to speak.

Youth 10 (lectern)

Sandals were important throughout the Old and New Testaments. Putting on sandals is often mentioned. In fact, it might seem odd to us to read constantly about people putting on or taking off their shoes. Actually these acts signified various things.

---

3. We found so many excellent Scriptures in the New Testament for "feet" that we chose to add a second New Testament reading.

4. This is a hymn that we simply sang as an anthem.

Youth 11

Putting on sandals was a sign of preparation for warfare. Putting on sandals was also a sign of preparation for a journey. Sandals were removed, however, when a person was in mourning. It was a sign of sadness, deprivation, and loss.

Youth 10

Sandals were a necessary part of a fine dress outfit, so the rich always wore them. However, sandals were not worn at all times. All footwear was removed when people went indoors, a practice we still find today in many parts of the world. Thus, the inside of a home or building was honored as a clean place. Dusty sandals stayed at the doorway. Sandals were also taken off in the temple and other sacred precincts. In New Testament times, it was a slave's task to remove or carry a master's shoes.

Youth 11

If we understand these specific rules, we can better understand the Second New Testament reading, which we just heard. There was great symbolic meaning when Jesus told his disciples to go and preach barefoot. This was against convention, especially when a person was outdoors or on a journey of any length.

Youth 10

Sandals played another quaint part in biblical times. There was an ancient practice that when a person bought or claimed title to a piece of land, he first walked around its boundaries or cast a shoe upon it. The Hebrew custom borrowed from this. Whenever there was a transfer of property, Hebrews would seal the deal with the symbolic exchange of a sandal.

Part II: Forgiveness

The following includes "echoes." Two people stand in the back or in the balcony and read the capitalized portions in unison.

This section requires two boys and one girl to act out the story. One boy is Jesus with at least a headdress and robe. The second is a Pharisee with a slightly more elegant headdress and robe. The girl needs a long robe and a long headdress that drapes as she leans forward.

The setting requires at minimum a table and two chairs.

Youth 12 (pulpit)

The second part of our Meditation is from Luke 7:36–50 and is about forgiveness.

One of the Pharisees asked Jesus to eat with him, and he went into the Pharisee's house and took a place at table.

Pause and wait for "Jesus" and the "Pharisee" to sit down.

And a woman in the city (A WOMAN IN THE CITY), who was a sinner (WHO WAS A SINNER), having learned that he was eating in the Pharisee's house, brought an alabaster jar of ointment (OF OINTMENT).

Pause and wait for the "woman" to enter and approach Jesus.

She stood behind him at his feet (AT HIS FEET), weeping, and began to bathe his feet with her tears (WITH HER TEARS), and to dry them with her hair (WITH HER HAIR). Then she continued kissing his feet (HIS FEET) and anointing them with the ointment (WITH THE OINTMENT).

Pause as the "woman" kneels by Jesus and bends slightly so her long headdress brushes the floor. Keep this gesture simple. Understatement is important. She need not make a lot of motion as if she's crying or wiping his feet.

Now when the Pharisee who had invited him saw this, he said to himself, "If this man were a prophet, he would have known who and what kind of woman this is who is touching him—that she is a sinner."

Jesus spoke up and said to him, "Simon, I have something to say to you."

"Teacher," he replied, "Speak."

"A certain creditor had two debtors; one owed five hundred denarii, and the other fifty. When they could not pay, he canceled the debts for both of them. Now which of them will love him more?"

Simon answered, "I suppose the one for whom he canceled the greater debt."

And Jesus said to him, "You have judged rightly."

Jesus reaches down, extends his hand to the woman, and helps her stand as he stands.

Then turning toward the woman, he said to Simon, "Do you see this woman? (THIS WOMAN?) I entered your house; you gave me no water for my feet (FOR MY FEET), but she has bathed my feet with her tears (WITH HER TEARS) and dried them with her hair (WITH HER HAIR). You gave me no kiss (GAVE ME NO KISS), but from the time I came in she has not stopped kissing my feet. You did not anoint my head with oil (WITH OIL), but she has anointed my feet with ointment (WITH OINTMENT).

Therefore, I tell you, her sins, which were many, have been forgiven; hence she has shown great love (SHOWN GREAT LOVE). But the one to whom little is forgiven, loves little." Then he said to her, "Your sins are forgiven." (YOUR SINS ARE FORGIVEN) . . . And he said to the woman, "Your faith has saved you; go in peace." (GO IN PEACE.)

*HYMN

"Jesu, Jesu, Fill Us with Your Love"
   Ghanaian folk melody

During the hymn, Youth 15 goes behind the screen with the microphone to be ready to read the "God" lines in next section.

Part III: Faith[5]

Youth 13 (pulpit)

For the third part of our Meditation, we will read a piece called "Footprints in the Sand."

One night a man had a dream. He dreamed he was walking along the beach with the Lord. Across the sky flashed scenes from his life.

For each scene, he noticed two sets of footprints in the sand—one belonging to him, and the other to the Lord. When the last scene of his life flashed before him, he looked back at the footprints in the sand. He noticed that many times along the path of his life there was only one set of footprints. He also noticed that it happened at the very lowest and saddest times in his life. This really bothered him, and he questioned the Lord about it.

Youth 14 (lectern)

"Lord, you said that once I decided to follow you, you would walk with me all the way. But I have noticed that during the most troublesome times in my life there is only one set of footprints. I don't understand why. When I needed you most you would leave me."

The Lord replied,

Youth 15 (from behind the screen with a microphone)

"My precious, precious child. I love you, and I would never leave you. During your times of trial and suffering, when you see only one set of footprints in the sand, it was then that I carried you."

ANTHEM

"Goin' Up Yonder"
  Walter Hawkins

Part IV: Greed[6]

Youth 16 (pulpit)

The fourth section of the Meditation is about Greed.

Youth 17 (at top of chancel steps with microphone)

We are salespeople. And we like to make money.

---

5. This section is quite sentimental, but the young people really wanted to include it. It is important to find a balance between sentiment and content. These can often clash in youth services.

6. Rarely do we include an actual play or a skit in the service. The main problem is the effort of rehearsing and getting youth to memorize lines. This is an example of a simple two-person skit, which, if necessary, could be read as the two stand at the pulpit or lectern.

Youth 18 (also at top of chancel steps with microphone)

To make money, you need a winning idea. You can look for something absolutely new and unusual, a fad or an invention (like calculators on your wristwatch or Barney ice cream).

Youth 17

Or, the other way is to latch on to an idea so basic to life that there will always be a market. Like barbers. Hair always grows. We will always need someone to cut it. There will always be money to be made as a barber.

Youth 18

Now, shoes and feet go together. Feet and shoes, shoes and feet. That was an opportunity that the two of us saw.

Youth 17

Everyone wants shoes, and so everyone needs us to sell them some.

Youth 18

And then sell them some more.

Youth 17

And more . . . and fashion helps, too.

Youth 18

Take, for example, these youth these days. We've asked some star athletes to wear our shoes and put their names on them. Then the youth get all pumped up about our pumped-up shoes.

Youth 17

They like high-steppin' shoes. With colors. They barely wear them and they need another pair. To match another outfit.

Youth 18

And we are happy to accommodate them. What's $70 or $100 for a pair of shoes? We love it.

Youth 17

Let's sell them some more!

Youth 18

But youth aren't the only market. We also like women and men who think about their looks a lot. What's $70 or $100 for a pair of shoes, right? We love it!

Youth 17

But selling shoes is not always easy. We have had our business cycles. Today we're doing great, but it wasn't always that way.

Youth 18

No it wasn't. There was a time when we ran into a really tough times.

Youth 17

Yeah, it was when Jesus was alive. It was those people around him—his disciples. Now, they were all screwed up. They completely missed the formula. Feet and shoes. Shoes and feet. Feet and shoes. They go together.

Youth 18

But they just didn't get it. They said that Jesus had told them to go unshod—unshod, barefoot! Can you believe that? When they were going out to preach the gospel and spread Jesus' word, when they were selling, so to speak, when they were on the road, hitting up the public—they refused to wear shoes. How crazy can you get!

Youth 17

I'm sure glad that didn't last long. It's much better these days. Let fashion be king! What's $70 or $100 anyway?

Part V: Celebration

Youth 19

To end our meditation, we will now share in a celebration song. With our theme of feet we have been able to explore customs and emotions. Feet are a humble part of our body, yet they carry us, serve us, and represent many of our human contradictions.

But, most important of all, feet allow us to dance and celebrate. For that reason, we end our mediation this morning with a song and dance. We invite you to remain sitting and sing with us the hymn "I Danced in the Morning."

HYMN

"I Danced in the Morning"
  American Shaker melody

Congregation remains seated.[7] On the refrain, all youth move around the sanctuary, find a child to be a dance partner, and twirl in the aisles with them.

CALL TO OFFERING[8]

OFFERTORY

"Jerusalem"
C. Hubert H. Parry

---

7. We kept everyone seated, although this is a lively song, so that they could see the children whirling in the aisles.

8. At this point many youth and children are returning to their seats. We did not use a regular "Call to Offering" because of the moving about. Instead, we had the offering plates at the back, and the ushers picked them up there.

*THE DOXOLOGY

*RECEIVING OF THE OFFERING

Youth 20

In receiving the offering, let us remember these words from Hebrews: Therefore lift your drooping hands and strengthen your weak knees, and make straight paths for your feet, so that what is lame may not be put out of joint, but rather be healed. Pursue peace with everyone, and the holiness without which no one will see the Lord (Hebrews 12:12–14).

PRAYERS OF THE PEOPLE

Youth 21 (lectern)

Please bow your heads for prayer.

Dear God, we pause now to pray. Our minds are focused, our hands are clasped, our feet are still. We pray today, for people who walk a path of courage, one of values, commitment, responsibility, honor, and love. This is often a lonely path. We pray that you be with each of us as we strive to walk that path.

We pray today for people who must walk. For those refugees who are fleeing violence, war, hunger, and strife. Be with them as they seek protection and a new life.

We pray today for people who cannot walk, who are lame, who suffer diseases that keep them immobile or moving stiffly or haltingly. Give them strength, patience, and comfort.

We pray today for those who work on their feet. For nurses, waitresses, and shop clerks. For mail carriers and flight attendants. For construction workers, sanitation workers, and schoolteachers. Help them to have stamina and energy.

We pray for those who are fleet of feet, for those who train and run fast in the pursuit of high performance in games and races. Teach them discipline, give them strength, and encourage them as they praise the physical abilities you gave to us.

And finally, we pray for all people as we begin life crawling on all fours, as we stand upright and walk on two feet, and as we eventually lean on canes and make three imprints in the sand. Be with us in all these times, and remind us constantly of Jesus Christ who taught us to pray . . .

THE LORD'S PRAYER

Congregation

Our Father, who art in heaven . . . .

*CLOSING HYMN

"Christ of the Upward Way"
George Lomas, 1876

*BENEDICTION

Youth (gathered at the chancel steps)

And now go forth into the world, with grace-filled steps and in peace.

Congregation

Together may we share the light of God's countenance upon us. May God bless you children, and keep you.

Youth

And may God bless you, too, O Children of God.

POSTLUDE

PROPS AND PARAPHERNALIA

The following is a list and description of the things needed in the service. We have organized them by the order required.

Entrance

We cut out large construction-paper footprints and stuck them on the sidewalk, steps, and entrance of the church. This alerted people that something was afoot with church that morning.

The Backdrop

We recycled the backdrop yet again. This time we took a couple

FEET

of the footprints that we used for the entrance and spraypainted their silhouettes onto the backdrop. We created a lively jumble of them.

Old Testament Reading

The three girls wore black leotards, tights, and head scarves to hide their hair and make them all look as similar or anonymous as possible. Each carried at least two fire-colored silky scarves.

Moses wore a simple robe, a tie at the waist, a headdress, and, most important, sandals. We made sure the sandals were easy to slip on and off. A nice addition is a shepherd staff.

Meditation: Part II—Forgiveness

It is important that this section be handled with understatement. The setting can be very simple with just two chairs and a small table. The boys wear long robes with ropes at the waist and headdresses that largely hide their faces. The girl wears a long robe and a veil that shadows her face. The veil can fall forward when she bends to suggest the long hair she uses to wipe Jesus' feet.

FEET

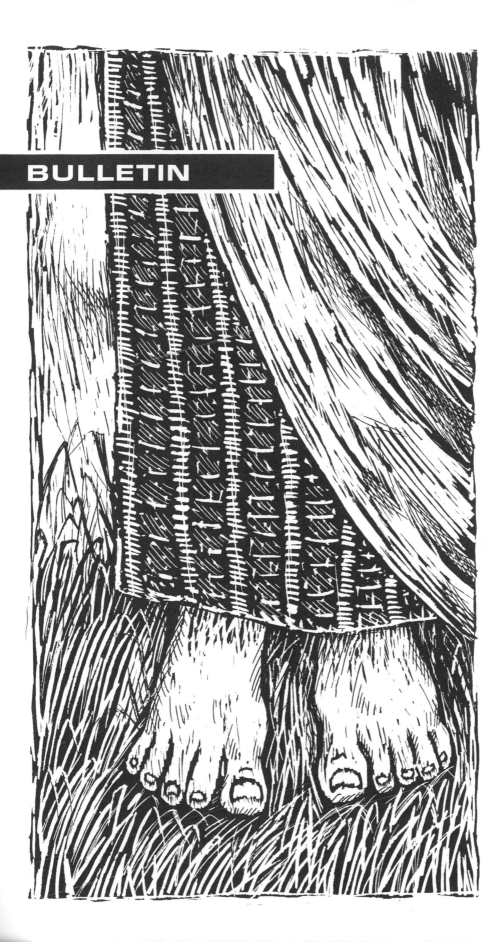

Please remove your shoes before entering the sanctuary.

PRELUDE

We invite you to consider the following passage while listening to the music of the Prelude. The Reading is from Psalm 99, verse 5.

> Extol the LORD our God;
>
> > worship at God's footstool.
> >
> > > Holy is God!

WORDS OF WELCOME

CHORAL INTROIT

"Alleluia, Alleluia! Give Thanks"
Donald Fishel, 1973

> Alleluia, alleluia, we walk in the path of God
>
> Alleluia, alleluia, we follow God's way.

UNISON CALL TO WORSHIP

Congregation
> Suddenly Jesus met them and said, "Greetings!" And they came to him, took hold of his feet, and worshiped him. (Matthew 28:9)

* PROCESSIONAL HYMN

"Praise, My Soul, the King of Heaven"
John Goss, 1869

*UNISON PRAYER OF ADORATION AND THANKSGIVING

Congregation
> We have come together today, O God, joined in the pathway of life that you have provided. We rejoice that in Jesus we have been taught to walk this path in peace, love, and harmony. We offer thanks that the challenges of this path, its twists, turns, and distance, are not for us to travel alone. You are our guide. You are our vista. You are our resting point. We are privileged to continue our journey with you, and in our hearts we are grateful. Amen.

ANTHEM

"I've Got a Robe"
Traditional

WORDS OF ASSURANCE

*GLORIA PATRI

TIME WITH ADULTS

"Make a Joyful Noise (with Our Feet)"

OLD TESTAMENT READING

Exodus 3:1–6

FIRST NEW TESTAMENT READING

Mark 1:12–13

*HYMN

"Jesus Walked This Lonesome Valley"
American spiritual

SECOND NEW TESTAMENT READING

Matthew 10:5, 9–14

ANTHEM

"Guide My Feet"
African-American spiritual

MEDITATIONS

Part I: Shoes and the Bible

Part II: Forgiveness

*HYMN

"Jesu, Jesu, Fill Us with Your Love"
Ghanaian folk melody

Part III: Faith

ANTHEM

"Goin' Up Yonder"
Walter Hawkins

Part IV: Greed

Part V: Celebration

HYMN

"I Danced in the Morning"
American Shaker melody

CALL TO OFFERING

OFFERTORY

"Jerusalem"
C. Hubert H. Parry

*THE DOXOLOGY

*RECEIVING OF THE OFFERING

PRAYERS OF THE PEOPLE

THE LORD'S PRAYER

*CLOSING HYMN

"Christ of the Upward Way"
George Lomas, 1876

*BENEDICTION

Youth

And now go forth into the world, with grace filled steps and in peace.

Congregation

Together may we share the light of God's countenance upon us. May God bless you children, and keep you.

Youth

And may God bless you, too, O Children of God.

POSTLUDE

*Those who are able, please stand.

WHEAT

CHAPTER 10

PRELUDE

We invite you to consider the following passage while listening to the music of the Prelude. Reading is from Psalm 81, verse 16:

> I would feed you with the finest of the wheat,
>
> and with honey from the rock I would satisfy you.

WORDS OF WELCOME   WHEAT

Youth 1 (pulpit)

The youth of _____ Church of _____ welcome you to this special time when the young people of the church plan and lead our worship.

Youth 2 (lectern)

Today we are exploring a simple and basic element of life: wheat. We have chosen this often unexciting, cheap, and common subject for two reasons. First, we have been all too aware this past year of the hunger in the world. Today we, the youth of this church, think of the children around the world and the nourishment that they need.

Youth 1

Second, wheat reminds us immediately of bread, which is a central element in our life together as a church. The breaking of bread is our Sacrament of Communion, and nourishes us on a spiritual level.

Youth 2

We invite you to join in the spirit of our worship today. This is an opportunity to stop and meditate on the underlying gifts in our life—gifts of nourishment, health, growth, and communion.

CALL TO WORSHIP

Youth 3 (back of sanctuary)

As we hear from Joel 2:23–24:

> O children of Zion, be glad and rejoice in the LORD your God; for he has given the early rain for your vindication, he has poured down for you abundant rain, the early and the later rain, as before. The threshing floors shall be full of grain, the vats shall overflow with wine and oil.

*PROCESSIONAL HYMN

"Guide Me, O Thou Great Jehovah"
John Hughes, 1907

---

*Those who are able to stand should do so for each part of the service marked with an asterisk.

*UNISON PRAYER OF CONFESSION

Youth 4 (lectern)

Let us join together reading the Unison Prayer of Confession as printed in the bulletin.

Congregation

Dear Lord and Provider, you have brought us great bounty and wealth. The earth through your magnificent generosity is abundant with fruit and grains. Yet we have squandered this earthly endowment. We waste food. We do not care for the land. We think of our own cravings and choices rather than the needs of your creation. We ask you to forgive us. Help us to honor, to respect, to conserve the glory of your nature. Teach us to plant, to raise, to harvest, to share your gifts to us and to give thanks. We ask this in the name of Jesus Christ. Amen.

ASSURANCE

Youth 5 (lectern)

From John 12:24 we know these words: Very truly, I tell you, unless a grain of wheat falls into the earth and dies, it remains just a single grain; but if it dies, it bears much fruit.

Believe what the Lord has said and follow in God's way.

*GLORIA PATRI

TIME WITH ADULTS

One youth leads. Seven act as ushers and pass through the congregation large baskets full of goldfish-shaped oyster crackers.

Youth 6 (standing informally at the front of the congregation)

For today's Time with Adults we are going to tell you a story from the Bible. This is a story of a miracle. We might not understand this story but we can certainly enjoy it and allow ourselves to wonder. Listen to the story, and when the basket is passed, help yourself. We intend that the contents of the story and the contents of the basket will feed you.

Youth 6 goes to Communion Table, picks up a Bible.

Youth 6

I read now from Matthew 15:32–38:

Then Jesus called his disciples to him and said, "I have compassion for the crowd, because they have been with me now for three days and have nothing to eat; and I do not want to send them away hungry, for they might faint on the way." The disciples said to him, "Where are we to get enough bread in the desert to feed so great a crowd?" Jesus asked them, "How many loaves have you?" They said, "Seven, and a few small fish." Then ordering the crowd to sit down on the ground, he took the seven loaves and the fish; and after giving thanks he broke them and gave them to the disciples, and the disciples gave them to the crowds. And all of them ate and were filled; and they took up the broken pieces left over, seven baskets full. Those who had eaten were four thousand men, besides women and children.

HYMN

"Sheaves of Summer"
Casáreo Gabaráin, 1973

Congregation remains seated, and the baskets continue to be passed until all are served.

FIRST NEW TESTAMENT READING

Youth 7 (lectern)

The First New Testament Reading today is taken from Mark 4:26–29.

He also said, "The kingdom of God is as if someone would scatter seed on the ground, and would sleep and rise night and day, and the seed would sprout and grow, he does not know how. The earth produces of itself, first the stalk, then the head, then the full grain in the head. But when the grain is ripe, at once he goes in with his sickle, because the harvest has come."

CHORAL INTERJECTION[1]

EXPLANATION

Youth 8 (pulpit)

This is one of the many parables Jesus told to teach us. This parable is one of the "contrast" parables. This means that in the story there is a huge contrast between tiny beginnings and enormous ends. In this case, the person scatters seeds on the land and then, totally oblivious to what is going on, he observes how the seeds turn into a ripe and ready harvest. Without being tended, the grain becomes an abundant field of wheat. In this way, Jesus is telling us of the kingdom's closeness and inevitability.

CHORAL INTERJECTION

SECOND NEW TESTAMENT READING

Youth 7 (lectern)

The second New Testament Reading for today is Matthew 13:3–9.

---

1. In this service we added an explanation or discussion to the Scripture readings. We separated these with a brief line of music from "Carol for All Seasons" done by the youth choir or the bell choir or both.

And he told them many things in parables, saying: "Listen! A sower went out to sow. And as he sowed, some seeds fell on the path, and the birds came and ate them up. Other seeds fell on rocky ground, where they did not have much soil, and they sprang up quickly, since they had no depth of soil. But when the sun rose, they were scorched; and since they had no root, they withered away. Other seeds fell among thorns, and the thorns grew up and choked them. Other seeds fell on good soil and brought forth grain, some a hundredfold, some sixty, some thirty. Let anyone with ears listen!"

CHORAL INTERJECTION

EXPLANATION

Youth 8

Two interpretations have been given to this parable. The first one is to treat it like an allegory. That means the reader assigns each element in the parable to mean something else. For example, the sower is Jesus, the seed is the word of God, and the various kinds of soils are the various kinds of listeners who receive the word of God. If we follow this train of thought, the parable becomes one that exhorts us. It tells us how to listen. It is a "dos and don'ts" lesson.

But, a better interpretation has been given. To many of us in the Western world, this story seems like an example of bad farming. It sounds like neglect to toss seeds onto all sorts of soils. In Palestine, however, sowing is the first step of planting. Plowing comes second. And so this parable becomes, like the first one we read, a contrast parable instead of an allegory. It is about the regular act of planting and the harvest that follows. It is about the many frustrations farmers can face while raising their crops. It describes also the abundant harvest. In short, Jesus is confident that God has made a beginning and that the kingdom will inevitably come.

CHORAL INTERJECTION

MEDITATIONS

Part I: The Gift

Youth 9 (pulpit)

The first half of our Meditation is titled The Gift. We refer to the psalms to guide us in our thoughts:

I read now from Psalm 147:14:

He grants peace within your borders;

he fills you with the finest of wheat.

Youth 10 (lectern)

Wheat is a simple food, a basic food, a nourishing food. Grains are at the beginning of our food chain. But we often substitute more expensive, more costly, and less healthful foods in our diets. We abandon or ignore the core gift we receive in wheat and grains. Consider some facts:

While the next question is read, two youth unroll large scroll down the center aisle. "Flip" it so each of the congregation can see what is written on it.

Youth 9

How many people will starve to death this year? *(Pause as scroll is being displayed.)* Sixty million!

Wait until the two youth remove the scroll from the aisle.

Youth 10

Consider a second fact. How many people could be fed annually by the grain and soybeans eaten by U.S. livestock?

Ten youth, standing in front of chancel, hold up placardlike signs with individual numbers on them that read: 1 300 000 000.

Youth 9

One billion, three hundred million.

Youth 10

Consider a third fact.

The same ten people regroup into a cluster or chorus that "answers" the questions posed by Youths 9 and 10.

Youth 9

How many pounds of potatoes can be grown on . . .

Youth 10

. . . one acre of land?

Chorus of 10

Twenty thousand pounds of potatoes.

Youth 9

How many pounds of beef can be produced on . . .

Youth 10

. . . one acre of land?

Chorus of 10

165 pounds of beef.

Youth 9

The earth is a gift; wheat is a gift; nourishment is a gift. To squander the simple gifts we have been given is to turn our backs on our God. It is only with God and from God that our hunger is satisfied.

*HYMN

"You Satisfy the Hungry Heart"
   Robert E. Kreutz, 1976

Part II: The Bread of Life

Youth 11 (pulpit)

The second part of the Meditation is about bread as sustenance for our life, both physical and spiritual.

If you are a child of Bosnia and you are hungry, where does your food come from? The stores are empty, the farms are burned, the battles are brutal, the people are scattered. Where might your food come from?

A plastic-foam airplane is released and descends on wire.

Youth 11

If you are a child of Somalia and you are hungry, where does your food come from? The land is dry, the crops are burned, the countryside is dangerous, the people are exhausted. Where might your food come from?

Three youth operate the large cardboard "truck." One holds the truck body, and the other two turn the wheels as it moves across the front of the sanctuary.

Youth 11

If you are a child of the streets of America, where does your food come from? Your home is a car, you see people eating ice cream, drinking from cans, munching chips from bags, but you have no money to buy. Where might your food come from?

Five youths stand as if in a "cafeteria" line. Three hold pots. The fourth "ladles" food onto the fifth's tin plate.

Youth 11

If you are a child of God, where does your food come from?

One youth stands behind the Communion Table and raises bread.

Youth 11

Jesus said to them, "I am the bread of life. Whoever comes to me will never be hungry, and whoever believes in me will never be thirsty."

ANTHEM

"Let Us Break Bread Together"[2]
   African-American spiritual

CALL TO OFFERING

Youth 12

Then the LORD said to Moses, "I am going to rain bread from heaven for you, and each day the people shall go out and gather enough for that day" (Exodus 16:4a).

---

2. This is a simple song that happens to be in our hymnbook. We used it here as an anthem to make a transition from the Meditation to the Offering.

So, too, shall we rain our bounty upon others so that they may share with us all the great and good things we have received.

Youth 12 hands offering plates to the ushers.

*OFFERTORY

*THE DOXOLOGY

*RECEIVING OF THE OFFERING

Youth 12

In receiving the offering, let us remember that the wheat and the leaven together will make a loaf, a loaf that rises while baking. It nourishes many.

PRAYERS OF THE PEOPLE

Youth 13 (lectern)

Let us bow now for prayer.

Dear Lord, we pray today for the children of the world who are hungry. We think of those in Somalia, in Bosnia-Herzegovina, in India, in Brazil, and here in our own country, our own state, and our own city. Help us to reach out, to share, and to solve this terrible and persistent problem of hunger in our world.

We pray also for the land from which our food comes. Nurture it with sun and rain. Coax the seeds to grow abundantly. Teach us to be good stewards of it. Help us live in a way that supports and cares for all nature.

We pray today for understanding. We have meditated on the symbol of wheat in a search for answers. What are the basic ingredients of our lives and how can we best offer them to you in service? Help us to grow, learn, and flourish so that we may continue to honor and worship you.

Be with us in all these times, and remind us constantly of Jesus Christ who taught us to pray . . .

THE LORD'S PRAYER

Congregation

Our Father, who art in heaven . . .

*CLOSING HYMN

"Come, Labor On"
Thomas Tertius Nobel, 1918

*BENEDICTION

Youth (gathered at the chancel steps)

And now go forth into the world in peace, sharing the bounty of the land with each other.

Congregation

Together may we share the light of God's countenance upon us. May God bless you children, and keep you.

Youth

And may God bless you, too, O Children of God.

POSTLUDE

PROPS AND PARAPHERNALIA

The following is a list and description of the things needed in the service. We have organized them by the order required.

Time with Adults

Prepare baskets with unfolded paper napkins in them filled with fish-shaped oyster crackers for passing through the congregation.

Meditation: Part I—The Gift

To make a large scroll, use the large butcher paper and roll it around two long poles the size of broom handles. Be sure the paper when unrolled is at least five feet long. The larger the better because it is unrolled down the aisle.

The next task is tedious. During a down time give the youth felt-tipped markers and have them make dozens and dozens of marks (four straight lines and a fifth one slashing across) on the "scroll" paper. Cover the paper with the marks. The point is to use a simple, enumerating symbol to show a very large number—which is still far away from the count of sixty million deaths a year from starvation.

Ten large squares of poster board or stiff paper. One has a large "1" painted on it. Another has a large "3" painted on it. The rest have "0." In the service ten people stand in a line formation and each holds up one sheet so that the large number 1,300,000,000 is "spelled out."

Meditation: Part II—The Bread of Life

You will need a large plastic-foam airplane. Ours had a three-foot wing span; it was a toy out of someone's basement. This could be constructed out of a large sheet of construction paper folded like a paper airplane.

We rigged it onto a wire hung from the upper back wall of the balcony. It stretched down diagonally across the congregation and was attached to the wall behind the pulpit. At this section in the service (we rehearsed this a lot to the glee of everyone), the plane was released from the balcony and sort of soared and floated down the wire and gracefully arrived at the pulpit, illustrating the Bosnian airlift.

Next, you will need a large cardboard truck-shaped cutout with rotating wheels. Our truck was large enough for three people to stand behind and "drive" across the front of the chancel. One person "carried" the truck, and two people rotated the big wheels. The concept was to rely on large geometry (big square cab, large round wheels, massive rectangular back/storage bed) to illustrate from a child's perspective the size and impressive nature of the big relief trucks used in Somalia.

You will also need big pots, ladles, and a tin plate. We borrowed these from the church kitchen and lined them up on a table to illustrate a soup kitchen, where the children of the streets of America find their food.

On the Communion Table, have displayed a communion chalice and a plate with a loaf of bread on it.

WHEAT

BULLETIN

WHEAT

PRELUDE

We invite you to consider the following passage while listening to the music of the Prelude. Reading is from Psalm 81, verse 16:

> I would feed you with the finest of the wheat,
>
> and with honey from the rock I would satisfy you.

WORDS OF WELCOME

CALL TO WORSHIP

*PROCESSIONAL HYMN

"Guide Me, O Thou Great Jehovah"
John Hughes, 1907

*UNISON PRAYER OF CONFESSION

Congregation

> Dear Lord and Provider, you have brought us great bounty and wealth. The earth through your magnificent generosity is abundant with fruit and grains. Yet we have squandered this earthly endowment. We waste food. We do not care for the land. We think of our own cravings and choices rather than the needs of your creation. We ask you to forgive us. Help us to honor, to respect, to conserve the glory of your nature. Teach us to plant, to raise, to harvest, to share your gifts to us and to give thanks. We ask this in the name of Jesus Christ. Amen.

ASSURANCE

*GLORIA PATRI

TIME WITH ADULTS

Matthew 15:32–38

HYMN

"Sheaves of Summer"
Casáreo Gabaráin, 1973

Congregation remains seated and the baskets continue to be passed until all are served.

FIRST NEW TESTAMENT READING

Mark 4:26–29

CHORAL INTERJECTION

EXPLANATION

CHORAL INTERJECTION

SECOND NEW TESTAMENT READING

Matthew 13:3–9

CHORAL INTERJECTION

EXPLANATION

CHORAL INTERJECTION

MEDITATIONS

Part I: The Gift

*HYMN

"You Satisfy the Hungry Heart"
> *Robert E. Kreutz, 1976*

Part II: The Bread of Life

ANTHEM

"Let Us Break Bread Together"
> *African-American spiritual*

CALL TO OFFERING

OFFERTORY

*THE DOXOLOGY

*RECEIVING OF THE OFFERING

PRAYERS OF THE PEOPLE

THE LORD'S PRAYER

*CLOSING HYMN

"Come, Labor On"
Thomas Tertius Nobel, 1918

*BENEDICTION

Youth

And now go forth into the world in peace, sharing the bounty of the land with each other.

Congregation

Together may we share the light of God's countenance upon us. May God bless you children, and keep you.

Youth

And may God bless you, too, O Children of God.

POSTLUDE

*Those who are able, please stand.

SWORDS

PRELUDE

We invite you to consider the following passage while listening to the music of the Prelude. Reading is from Isaiah 49, verses 1 to 2.

The LORD called me before I was born,

while I was in my mother's womb he named me.

He made my mouth like a
sharp sword,

SWORDS

in the shadow of his hand he hid me.

WORDS OF WELCOME

Youth 1 (pulpit)
The youth of _____ Church of _____ welcome you to this special time during which the young people of the church plan and lead our worship.

Youth 2 (lectern)
This year we are saddened, concerned, and dismayed by the increasing violence in our world, our nation, our community, and our own streets. We feel the need to meditate, to pray, to explore this problem. Therefore, we have chosen swords as our theme for this year's service.

Youth 1
We invite you to join in the spirit of our worship today. Through our worship together we hope to give a voice to the fears and concerns that are part of our shared life as young and old people, as citizens, and as Christians. Rather than divide us, we earnestly wish that swords today will unite us.

CALL TO WORSHIP

Youth 3 (back of sanctuary)
Hear the words of King David, reading from Psalm 144:

I will sing a new song to you, O God; upon a ten-stringed harp I will play to you, the one who gives victory to kings, who rescues his servant David. Rescue me from the cruel sword, and deliver me from the hand of aliens, whose mouths speak lies, and whose right hands are false. May our sons in their youth be like plants full grown, our daughters like corner pillars, cut for the building of a palace. . . . Happy are the people to whom such blessings fall; happy are the people whose God is the LORD!

*PROCESSIONAL HYMN

"Come, Thou Almighty King"
Felice de Giardini, 1769

---

*Those who are able to stand should do so for each part of the service marked with an asterisk.

UNISON PRAYER

Youth 4 (lectern)

Let us join together in the Unison Prayer, and recite the words from the hymn "When Will People Cease Their Fighting?" by C. Hubert H. Parry, 1897.

RESPONSE

Youth 5 (lectern)

From Matthew 26:52 we hear these words of Jesus: Put your sword back into its place; for all who take the sword will perish by the sword.

Believe what the Lord has said and follow in his way. Amen.

*GLORIA PATRI

TIME WITH ADULTS

Youth 6 (informally standing at the "police display" table in front)

We have here on display a cache of toys and weapons. These are not real weapons—these are all toys and belong to the families of this church. Take a brief look at some of them: Here is a _____; and here is _____. This one is a well-used_____, etc.

At the end of the service, please pass by this table and look over this collection, this stash of play weapons.

Youths 7 and 8 start to pass the baskets with the "flip" books.

Youth 6

We are now passing out another little toy. This is a child's "flip book" that we have made. It is for you to keep. You take the book and flip through the pages and watch the image change. On the front is a sword; as you flip, it becomes a plowshare. In this child's book, a weapon becomes a tool—a tool for planting seeds, raising food, feeding the world. Keep this. Play with this and be reminded of its message.

*HYMN

"A Day of Peace"
C. Hubert H. Parry, 1916

OLD TESTAMENT READING

Youths 9, 10, 11, 12, 13, 14 form obvious line waiting their turn to read from the lectern. Create a feeling of prompt, no nonsense, orderliness. When your reading is finished, return to the line.

Youth 9

We have chosen short readings from the first six chapters of the Old Testament. Reading from Genesis 34:25–26:

On the third day, when they were still in pain, two of the sons of Jacob, Simeon and Levi, Dinah's brothers, took their swords and came against the city unawares, and killed all the males.

Youth 10

Reading from Exodus 15:9:

The enemy said, "I will pursue, I will overtake, I will divide the spoil, my desire shall have its fill of them. I will draw my sword, my hand shall destroy them."

Youth 11

Reading from Leviticus 26:7–8:

You shall give chase to your enemies, and they shall fall before you by the sword. Five of you shall chase to a hundred, and a hundred of you shall chase to ten thousand; your enemies shall fall before you by the sword.

Youth 12

Reading from Numbers 14:43:

For the Amalekites and the Canaanites will confront you there, and you shall fall by the sword; because you have turned back from following the LORD, the LORD will not be with you.

Youth 13

Reading from Deuteronomy 13:15:

. . . you shall put the inhabitants of that town to the sword, utterly destroying it and everything in it—even putting its livestock to the sword.

Youth 14

Reading from Joshua 10:30:

The LORD gave it also and its king into the hand of Israel; and he struck it with the edge of the sword, and every person in it; he left no one remaining in it; and he did to its king as he had done to the king of Jericho.

All six readers return to their seats at the same time.

NEW TESTAMENT READING

Youth 15 (lectern)

The New Testament Reading today is Ephesians 6:13–17. Unlike the Old Testament readings, which are stories of battles, combat, and war, this reading talks about weapons and armor in a more literary way. Here the sword is a simile.

Therefore take up the whole armor of God, so that you may be able to withstand on that evil day, and having done everything, to stand firm. Stand therefore, and fasten the belt of truth around your waist, and put on the breastplate of righteousness. As shoes for your feet put on whatever will make you ready to proclaim the gospel of peace. With all of these, take the shield of faith, with which you will be able to quench all the flaming arrows of the evil one. Take the helmet of salvation, and the sword of the Spirit, which is the word of God.

ANTHEM

"Down by the Riverside"
> *Spiritual*

MEDITATIONS

Part I: Guidance from the Bible: The Old Testament

Youth 16 (pulpit)

The first part of the Meditation is about the guidance we receive from the Old Testament. Swords were the weapons of biblical times. Those were not the days of guns, tanks, switchblades, bombs, stun guns, and all the other artillery of modern life. Weapons were simple. They were used in close combat; a person would fight face to face with another person.

Swords are mentioned by name approximately 442 times in the Bible.

Youths 17 and 18 stand in chancel and open up a "fan" of swords.

We looked in a Bible concordance and counted. This isn't surprising when you consider the numbers of assassinations, executions, fights, skirmishes, massacres, battles, and wars that are covered in the Old Testament. Much of the Old Testament story is about a small, struggling nation trying to establish and secure itself, its kings, and its temple.

Youths 17 and 18 lower the "fan."

However, the Old Testament is also a collection of contrasts. While Israel struggles for its life, we also read of the promise of God, of a life under God's undisputed reign. This contrast between the historic struggle of Israel and the promise of God can be and indeed is startling. We share a particularly sharp contrast with you now.

Youth 19 (standing tall on a bench on the right side of chancel)

Reading from Joel 3, verses 9 to 10. And Joel said:

Proclaim this among the nations: Prepare war, stir up the warriors. Let all the soldiers draw near, let them come up. Beat your plowshares into swords, and your pruning hooks into spears; let the weakling say, "I am a warrior."

Youth 20 (standing tall on bench on the left side of chancel)

Reading from Micah 4, verse 3: And Micah said:

He shall judge between many peoples, and shall arbitrate between strong nations far away; they shall beat their swords into plowshares, and their spears into pruning hooks; nation shall not lift up sword against nation, neither shall they learn war any more.

Part II: Guidance from the Bible: The New Testament

Youth 21 (pulpit)

The second part of the Meditation is about the guidance we gain from the New Testament. When we looked up the number of citations of swords in the Bible, most were in the Old Testament. Of the 442 quotes, only 36 were in the New Testament.

Jesus was the Prince of Peace. He was a healer and a teacher, not a warr. He spoke out against violence. He lived a life of peace. For example, let's review one story about him found in Luke 22. In this incident, Jesus was speaking and Judas brought a crowd near him. The disciples became nervous and said, "Lord, should we strike with the sword?" Then one of them struck the slave of the high priest and cut off his right ear. But Jesus said, "No more of this!" And he touched his ear and healed him (vs. 49–51).

Stories of violence are in both the Old and New Testaments. There are also important messages of peace and the kingdom of God where violence has no place. The message from Jesus is that love will reign, that love will overcome the violence, the blood, and crucifixion. We can find peace.

Part III: Guidance from the World around Us

Youth 22 (pulpit)

Finally in our Meditation we look for guidance from the world around us. As we have heard, the Bible is a book full of violent events. In the same way, life around us today does that, too. Violence is all around us. We showed you the toys that we as families of this church own. Here are the names of the toy weapons you can buy here by just going over to the mall or to most stores.

Youths 22 and 23 (pulpit and lectern) read the following lists alternating between each other.

Six youths unfurl the streamers and walk quickly (so the streamers flutter behind them) up and down the aisles during the reading.

Battle Clash Video Game	Final Flight Video
Terminator Computer Game	Hook Sword
Mini Blaster Gun	Gun Force Video
Cyber Blaster Gun	Crocodile Knife Sword
20 Super Soaker Gun	Biometal Video Game
SWAT Set Gun	Dark Speed Computer Game
Pirate Cutlass Sword	World of Zeen Computer Game

Armed Forces Gun Set

Demons Gaze Game

Terminator Rampage
Computer Game

Power Shooter Gun

Robin Hood Crossbow

Ripper Water Gun

Tidal Force 3 Gun

Super Stick Blaster Gun

Ultimate Weapon Set

American West Six Shooter for
Girls

Stinger Gun

Power Shooter 8-in-1 Gun

Bazooka Gun

Thunder Strike Gun

X–1000 Water Gun

Alien vs. Predator Video Game

Explorer Gun

Bomberman Video Game

Ninja Crossbow Sword

Fazor Flexor Gun

Ariel Assault Video

Dark Seed Video Game

Sewer Snark Computer Game

Sponge Blaster Gun

Strike Commander Video Game

Sonic Laser Gun

Terminator 2 Video Game

Nintendo Super Soaker Gun

Street Combat Video Game

Mech Warrior Video Game

Battle Cars Video Game

Dinosaur Flying Target

Strike Gunner Video

Ninja Shadow Warrior Sword

Pulsator Water Gun

Mighty Sounds Sword

World of Zeon Game

Mortal Combat Video Game

Neon Uzi Gun

Youth 22

We know our civilization cannot survive if violence and weapons are the primary way of solving problems. We need to learn other ways of using power that do not require modern swords. We need to learn to negotiate, communicate, share, and love.

Youth 23

But this doesn't simply happen. These are lifelong lessons to be learned. We must study, meditate upon, practice, and train in the methods of peace. Peace requires hard work, examples, skills, and steadfastness.

Youth 22

We are the children of the world. We know we are vulnerable to the violence of the world around us; and we must become strong.

Youth 23

How will this happen? We need you to teach us and each other about peace— to show in concrete, daily ways the methods of peace. We ask that each of you take a card from the pew racks, and while you are listening to the anthem, write a suggestion for how you can and will pass on the skills of peace. You need not sign your card. We hope that by writing down an idea a person can make a new commitment toward a life of peace. Please place your cards in the offering plates along with your offering.

ANTHEM

"Let There Be Peace on Earth"
Sy Miller & Jill Jackson, 1955

CALL TO OFFERING

Youth 24

Offer your gifts unto God; those of money; those of time; those of talent; those of love, that we may begin the work of peace on earth, today and always.

Youth 24 hands the offering plates to the ushers.

OFFERTORY

*THE DOXOLOGY

*RECEIVING OF THE OFFERING

Youth 24

In receiving the offering, we ask, O Lord, that you accept our gifts and melt and mold them not into weapons of violence but plowshares of peace. Amen.

PRAYERS OF THE PEOPLE

Youth 25 (pulpit)

Let us bow now for prayer.

Dear Lord, We come to you today in pain, in fear. We are living in a world torn apart by violence. Children die daily in terrible wars around the world. They also die daily in our schools, on our playgrounds, and in our streets. We are so afraid. We are so scared.

We are unsure. We do not know how to see a vision of peace. All around us different images insert themselves into our lives through our books, our televisions, our music, and language. We must learn to see your message of peace. Help us to see and to know.

We are unskilled. Even though we believe in peace, we do not know how to create peace. Teach us. Give us the abilities and the skills to be peaceful, to find other ways of solving problems and expressing ourselves.

Be with us. Lead us to the life of sharing, of health, of bounty, and of peace. Be with us, and remind us constantly of Jesus Christ who taught us to pray . . .

THE LORD'S PRAYER

Congregation

Our Father, who art in heaven . . .

*CLOSING HYMN

"Lead On, O King Eternal"
Henry Thomas Smart, c. 1835

*BENEDICTION

Youth (gathered at the chancel steps)

And now go forth into the world, not in violence but in peace.

Congregation

May God bless you, children, and keep you ever safe and in peace.

Youth

And may God bless you, too, O Children of God.

POSTLUDE

PROPS AND PARAPHERNALIA

The following is a list and description of the things needed in the service. We have organized them by the order required.

Entrance

The youth, along with some adults, built a simple, three-sided wooden frame about the size and shape of a door frame. They covered it with aluminum foil and rigged up green and red lights across the top. This apparatus was placed at the entrance to the sanctuary and acted like a metal detector, the kind found at airports. Everyone entering the sanctuary stepped through the security portal.

SWORDS

Decorations

A startling way to drive home our points about violence was to collect and display the toys of the children of the church that involve a violent theme. We covered a table with a white sheet, laid out the toys with labels such as "guns" or "swords" or "videos," etc. The effect was a police-raid display.

Time with Adults

During this section we handed out an alternative toy, a nonviolent toy which was a flip book. We made very simple ones by photocopying a series of pictures that were drawn by a youth. We then cut and stapled them so a person could "fan" through them and see the sword picture turn into a plowshare (see page 109).

Meditation: Part I—Guidance from the Bible, The Old Testament

To create a sense of many weapons, we cut sixteen long cardboard swords with various shaped handles that the youth individually decorated. We mounted the swords in the pattern of a fan on two large cardboard displays sheets, eight swords on each sheet of cardboard. They were held up during this section of the Meditation.

Meditation: Part III—Guidance from the World Around Us

As a way of dramatizing the lengthy list of violence-based toys, we created eight pairs of streamers. We made these four- to five-foot lengths of crepe-paper and tongue depressors. On the crepe-paper strips we wrote with felt-tipped markers in bold letters the names of the toys being read. We attached the paper strips to the tongue depressors, which acted as wands. The youth marched up and down the center and side aisles waving their streamers, as "waves" of toy names could be seen by the congregation.

The Offering

Place cards in the pews on which people can write their "peace skills" to place in the offering plates.

SWORDS

BULLETIN

PRELUDE

We invite you to consider the following passage while listening to the music of the Prelude. Reading from Isaiah 49, verses 16 through 26:

> The LORD called me before I was born,
>
> > while I was in my mother's womb he named me.
>
> He made my mouth like a sharp sword,
>
> > in the shadow of his hand he hid me.

WORDS OF WELCOME

CALL TO WORSHIP

*PROCESSIONAL HYMN

"Come, Thou Almighty King"
> *Felice de Giardini, 1769*

UNISON PRAYER

Let us join together in the Unison Prayer, and recite the words from the hymn "When Will People Cease Their Fighting?" by C. Hubert H. Parry, 1897.

RESPONSE

*GLORIA PATRI

TIME WITH ADULTS

*HYMN

"A Day of Peace"
C. Hubert H. Parry, 1916

OLD TESTAMENT READING

Genesis 34:25–26

Exodus 15:9

Leviticus 26:7–8

Numbers 14:43

Deuteronomy 13:15

Joshua 10:30

NEW TESTAMENT READING

Ephesians 6:13–17

ANTHEM

"Down by the Riverside"
Spiritual

MEDITATIONS

Part I: Guidance from the Bible: The Old Testament

Part II: Guidance from the Bible: The New Testament

Part III: Guidance from the World around Us

ANTHEM

"Let There Be Peace on Earth"
Sy Miller & Jill Jackson, 1955

CALL TO OFFERING

OFFERTORY

*THE DOXOLOGY

*RECEIVING OF THE OFFERING

PRAYERS OF THE PEOPLE

THE LORD'S PRAYER

*CLOSING HYMN

"Lead On, O King Eternal"
Henry Thomas Smart, c. 1835

*BENEDICTION

Youth
>And now go forth into the world, not in violence but in peace.

Congregation
>May God bless you, children, and keep you ever safe and in peace.

Youth
>And may God bless you, too, O Children of God.

POSTLUDE

*Those who are able, please stand.

WIND

PRELUDE

We invite you to consider the following passage while listening to the music of the Prelude. Reading is from Psalm 135, verse 7:

> He it is who makes the clouds rise at the end of the earth;
>> he makes lightnings for the rain
>> and brings out the wind
>>> from his storehouses.

WIND

WORDS OF WELCOME

Youth 1 (pulpit)

The youth of _____ Church of _____ welcome you to this special time during which the young people of the church plan and lead our worship.

Youth 2 (lectern)

It is the year _____ and we are closing in on (have reached) the millennium. Huge changes are sweeping our town, country, and world. It is as if a great wind is sweeping through our lives. Just imagine how members of our own church experience this future world.

Youth 1

There are people among us who hoist satellites into space. Toddlers play games on CD-ROMS. Many of us use the Internet, have car phones, depend on call waiting, and get cash at bank machines.

Youth 2

We are being blown into the future by technology. It is as powerful as the huge winds were in biblical times.

Youth 1

Thinking about these kinds of things, we chose wind as our theme.

Youth 2

Our service is about the powerful winds in our lives and in the lives of those in the Bible.

Youth 1

It is also about the small gusts, the little puffs that cool our faces, which bring us the fragrance of spring and the sprinkle of snowflakes.

Youth 2

We invite you to engage with us today in our service about wind.

CALL TO WORSHIP

Youth 3 (back of sanctuary)

Reading from Matthew 11:7–10:

As they went away, Jesus began to speak to the crowds about John: "What did you go out into the wilderness to look at? A reed shaken by the wind? What then did you go out to see? Someone dressed in soft robes? Look, those who wear soft robes are in royal palaces. What then did you go out to see? A prophet? Yes, I tell you, and more than a prophet. This is the one about whom it is written, 'See, I am sending my messenger ahead of you, who will prepare your way before you.'"

*PROCESSIONAL HYMN

"All Creatures of Our God and King"
Geistliche Kirchengesäng, 1623

*UNISON PRAYER OF CONFESSION

Youth 4 (lectern)

As we join together in reading the Unison Prayer of Confession, we suggest the following. We will read a section together. Then we will stop, and we ask that each person exhale a long, slow breath.

Youth 5 (pulpit)

Listen to the rushing sound as the whole congregation blows out. Each time we do this, imagine your breath, first as darker, smoky, polluted air.

Youth 4

With each exhaling, imagine your breath becoming clearer and more clean.

Youth 5

Keeping these instructions in mind, let us join together in reading the Unison Prayer of Confession as printed in the bulletin. *(Pause a moment.)*

Congregation

Dear Lord, We hear the words of the prophet Jeremiah in Jeremiah 5:12–13: They have spoken falsely of the Lord, and have said, "He will do nothing. No evil will come upon us, and we shall not see sword or famine" . . . *(stop and breathe)*

"The prophets are nothing but wind, for the word is not in them. Thus shall it be done to them!" . . . *(stop and breathe)*

We confess that we have heard the words but we have not listened . . . *(stop and breathe)*

We listen to false prophets; we speak falsely ourselves . . . *(stop and breathe)*

Open our hearts, our minds, and cleanse us. *(stop and breathe)*

We ask this in the name of Jesus Christ. Amen.

---

*Those who are able to stand should do so for each part of the service marked with an asterisk.

ASSURANCE

Youth 6 (lectern)

From Genesis 8, verse 1, we know these words: But God remembered Noah and all the wild animals and all the domestic animals that were with him in the ark. And God made a wind blow over the earth, and the waters subsided.

Believe what God has said and follow in God's way.

*GLORIA PATRI

TIME WITH ADULTS

Youth 7 (pulpit)

This part of our Sunday morning worship service is a special mini-sermon. Today we will be using a passage from Job 27:19–23.

All youth are involved in this. The seating is as follows: Youths 9 and 10, dressed in black, sit on chairs on each side of the chancel as if they are stagehands, ready to move across the "stage" quickly and rearrange items. Youths 11, 12, 13, and 14 sit behind the table holding their scarves out of sight. The rest of the youth sit in the choir lofts (along each side of the chancel so they are facing each other across the table.)

The only props/scenery[1] at the beginning is the long table in the middle of the chancel, covered with a huge white sheet so you cannot see the legs of the four youth sitting behind it.

Youth 8

They go to bed with wealth,

Wait as Youth 9 sets up the "riches." This means laying out pillows on one end and placing the "riches" on the opposite end.

Youth 7

They go to bed with wealth,

Wait as Youth 10 places the large doll and gold blanket on the table as if putting a person to bed.

Youth 8

but will do so no more;

Youth 7

but will do so no more;

Youth 8

they open their eyes and it is gone.

---

1. Remember that for fuller details on the props refer to the Props and Paraphernalia section at the end of each script.

Youth 9 quickly removes the riches off the table.

Youth 7

they open their eyes and it is gone.

Youth 10 quickly removes the blanket off the doll, replaces it with burlap, and exchanges the pillows with a large brick.

Youth 8

Terror overtakes them like a flood;

Youth 7

in the night a whirlwind carries them off.

Youth 8

The east wind lifts them up and they are gone;

Youths 11, 12, 13, and 14 stand at their chairs and begin to wave their long scarves in the air, making them flap and flutter.

Youth 7

it sweeps them out of their place.

Youth 8

It hurls at them without pity;

Youth 7

It hurls at them without pity;

Youth 8

they flee from its power in headlong flight.

Youth 7

they flee from its power in headlong flight.

Youth 9 darts forward, lifts the doll, and pitches it "off stage" for Youth 10 to catch and quickly put out of sight. Youths 11, 12, 13, and 14 stop waving scarves and sit down.

Youth 8

It claps its hands at them,

All youth start to clap.

Youth 7

It claps its hands at them,

Youth 8

and hisses at them from its place.

All youth stop clapping and start to hiss.

Youth 7

and hisses at them from its place.

All youth keep hissing until the last word.

OLD TESTAMENT READING

Youth 15 (lectern)

The Old Testament Reading today is from Exodus 14:21–22 and 15:9–10.

Then Moses stretched out his hand over the sea. The LORD drove the sea back by a strong east wind all night, and turned the sea into dry land; and the waters were divided. The Israelites went into the sea on dry ground, the waters forming a wall for them on their right and on their left.

The enemy said, "I will pursue, I will overtake, I will divide the spoil, my desire shall have its fill of them. I will draw my sword, my hand shall destroy them."

You blew with your wind, the sea covered them; they sank like lead in the mighty waters.

NEW TESTAMENT READING

Youth 16 (lectern)

The New Testament Reading today is Mark 4:35–41.

On that day, when evening had come, he said to them, "Let us go across to the other side." And leaving the crowd behind, they took him with them in the boat, just as he was. Other boats were with him. A great windstorm arose, and the waves beat into the boat, so that the boat was already being swamped. But he was in the stern, asleep on the cushion; and they woke him up and said to him, "Teacher, do you not care that we are perishing?" He woke up and rebuked the wind, and said to the sea, "Peace! Be still!" Then the wind ceased, and there was a dead calm. He said to them, "Why are you afraid? Have you still no faith?" And they were filled with great awe and said to one another, "Who then is this, that even the wind and the sea obey him?"

MEDITATIONS

Youth 17 (pulpit)

Wind is one of the great metaphors in the Bible. The prophets use wind to describe the glory and the power of God. New Testament stories are full of wind.

Youth 18 (lectern)

The wind swirls through the Bible. It also swirls around us today. We think of that old saying, "What goes around comes around." Wind is often first one thing and then another. To think about the wind is to think about contrasts. Our Meditation today will focus on the way the wind tells us about contrasts in the Bible. The first examples are how it both invites and destroys.

Part I: Invites and Destroys

Youth 17

In Ezekial 19:12 we hear how the wind *destroys*:

Loud noise on drums

Youth 18

But [the vine] was plucked up in fury, cast down to the ground; the east wind dried it up; its fruit was stripped off, its strong stem was withered; the fire consumed it.

Youth 17

In Song of Solomon 4:16, the wind *invites*:

Light and gentle trill on flute or violin

Youth 18

Awake, O north wind, and come, O south wind! Blow upon my garden that its fragrance be wafted abroad. Let my beloved come to his garden, and eat its choicest fruits.

Youth 17

In Job 21:18, again, the wind *destroys*:

Again, loud noise on drums

Youths 17 and 18

How often are they like straw before the wind, and like chaff that the storm carries away?

Part II: Power and Nothingness

Before Youth 18 reads the next section, Youths 19–25 should take their places.

Youth 18

Our second section is about another set of contrasts: the way the wind represents at times power and at times nothingness.

Youth 17

In Proverbs 11:29 the wind is nothingness.

Youths 19, 20, 21, 22 (in unison on chancel steps facing congregation but whispering)

Those who trouble their households will inherit wind, and the fool will be servant to the wise.

Youth 18

In Psalm 135:7, the wind is about power.

Youths 23, 24, 25 (in unison, standing midway in the center aisle, speaking very loudly)

He it is who makes the clouds rise at the end of the earth; he makes lightnings for the rain and brings out the wind from his storehouses.

Youth 17

In Isaiah 41:29, the wind is about nothingness.

Youths 19, 20, 21, 22 (again in unison from chancel, whispering)

No, they are all a delusion; their works are nothing; their images are empty wind.

* HYMN

"How Great Thou Art"
Swedish folk melody

Part III: Beginnings and Ends

Youth 18

And for the third section of the Meditation, we are reminded that the wind represents both beginnings and endings in the Bible. First we consider the beginnings of the church with the story of the Pentecost in Acts 2.

Youth 17

When the Day of Pentecost had come, they were all together in one place. And suddenly from heaven there came a sound like the rush of a violent wind, and it filled the entire house where they were sitting.

The "fire" descends from back of the sanctuary on wire.

Divided tongues, as of fire, appeared among them, and a tongue rested on each of them. All of them were filled with the Holy Spirit and began to speak in other languages, as the Spirit gave them ability.

* HYMN

"Wind Who Makes All Winds That Blow"
Joseph Parry, 1879

Youth 17

Next we consider our being mortal as we are reminded in Psalm 103:15–18.

All youth except the readers and Youths 24 and 25 stand in chancel, backs to congregation, holding "grass," "flowers," and pinwheels.

Youth 18

As for mortals, their days are like grass.

Youth in chancel hold up "grass" high overhead and wave gently back and forth.

Youth 17

As for mortals, their days are like grass[2]

Youth 18

they flourish like a flower of the field;

Youth in chancel hold up "flowers" as well and again wave gently as if in a breeze.

Youth 17

they flourish like a flower of the field;

Youths 17 and 18

for the wind passes over it, and it is gone, and its place knows it no more.

Slowly wave both "grass" and "flowers" in large arch downward. Bend over at the waist slowly until grass and flowers touch the floor. Let them fall quietly out of your hands.

Youths 23 and 24 enter with two babies from nursery and walk down the aisles so the babies can see the congregation and vice versa.

Youth 18

But the steadfast love of the LORD is from

everlasting to everlasting on those who fear him

and his righteousness to

children's children.

Youth in chancel hold up pinwheels high overhead and turn toward congregation.

Youth 17

to those who keep his covenant and remember to do his commandments.

Youth 18

to those who keep his covenant and remember to do his commandments.

CALL TO OFFERING

Youth 25

I say to you now from Ecclesiastes 1:6:

The wind blows to the south, and goes round to the north; round and round goes the wind, and on its circuits the wind returns.

So, too, with your wealth and your money. Give that you shall receive. We shall now collect the morning's offering.

Youth 25 hands the offering plates to the ushers.

---

2. We repeated each line because the passage is short, and we wanted to give enough time to express the message.

*THE DOXOLOGY

*RECEIVING OF THE OFFERING

Youth 25

Amos 4:13 reads:

For lo, the one who forms the mountains, creates the wind, reveals his thoughts to mortals, makes the morning darkness, and treads on the heights of the earth—the Lord, the God of hosts, is his name!

In that Name, we make these offerings.

*HYMN

"Every Time I Feel the Spirit"
African-American spiritual

PRAYERS OF THE PEOPLE AND THE YOUTH[3]

Youth 26 (pulpit)

Let us pray.

Dear Lord, as John 3:8 reminds us: The wind blows where it chooses, and you hear the sound of it, but you do not know where it comes from or where it goes. So it is with everyone who is born of the Spirit.

Today, we therefore offer you individual and corporate prayers. Let them be born on the wind and reach you with favor.

We pray today, O God, for our families . . .

Release a couple of balloons.

For children. Those who need food. Those who need housing. Those who are in families where there is pain.

Release a couple of balloons.

We pray for all of us that we may no longer be tossed to and fro and carried about with every wind of doctrine.

Release a couple of balloons.

We pray that each breath we draw will be a healthy one and each word we speak will be spoken with honesty and caring.

Release a couple of balloons.

We pray that the Spirit of the Lord will fill us.

---

3. These prayers were written by the youth. During one of the youth fellowship hours, we passed out notecards and asked each person to write a prayer. We consolidated these into the Prayers for the service.

Release a couple of balloons.

Be with us in all these times, and remind us constantly of Jesus Christ who taught us to pray . . .

THE LORD'S PRAYER

Congregation

Our Father, who art in heaven . . .

*CLOSING HYMN

"Breathe on Me, Breath of God"
Robert Jackson, 1894

*BENEDICTION

Youth (gathered at the chancel steps)

And now go forth into the world filled with the rush of the Spirit of God and in peace.

Congregation

Together may we share the light of God's countenance upon us. May God bless you children, and keep you.

Youth

And may God bless you, too, O Children of God.

CHORAL BENEDICTION

"Irish Benediction"

POSTLUDE

The following is a list and description of the things needed in the service. We have organized them by the order required.

Decorations

Using straws, construction paper, and folder pins, we made pinwheels. We put them in flower vases around the sanctuary.

Time with Adults

For this section we chose to tell a story. This one is filled with sounds (hisses and clapping) but requires minimum action; the character mostly sleeps.

WIND

The setting requires a long table in the chancel with a cloth covering it so the legs of the youth sitting behind it are screened.

The Doll

Plan to use lots of big safety pins. We pinned together socks, pants or skirt, and a T-shirt, which we stuffed with newspapers. We dressed this figure in a long robe and bright sash. For a head we created a ball of newspapers, covered it with light brown cloth, tied on an elaborate turban, and pinned this to the body.

The Bed and Riches

On the table we placed massive pillows at one end, some covered with embroidered gold (or something fancy) material. The doll was placed in a reclining position on the pillows. We laid a beautiful piece of silk cloth over it. At the feet we placed a collection of "riches" brought in by the youth: brass candlesticks, silver teapots, and other items.

When the wealth disappeared, a couple of youth dressed in black like stagehands moved quickly to replace the pillows with an ordinary brick. They also removed the fancy material, covered the doll with burlap, and removed the riches.

Scarves

We collected four or five lengths of cloth and long scarves that the young people waved and flapped to indicate blowing wind.

Meditation

To demonstrate the contrasts, one youth brought some snare drums, another brought a violin (could have been a flute or other instrument for a melodic and gentle sound).

For grass, each twisted together a couple of green pipe cleaners to make yard-long "stalks of grass." Each made a handful that they could wave overhead.

For flowers we used a couple of sheets of tissue paper, folded like a fan, pinched in the center with a staple, and then fluffed to form a blossom. Many craft suggestions for making flowers are available. Aim for large, colorful blossoms that can be seen clearly from the back of the room.

Babies

We arranged for two youths to go to the nursery and pick up two infants for a brief parade down the sanctuary aisles. Other youth waved a few pinwheels to entertain them.

Pentecost flames

Our Pentecost flames were a little crude but captured the attention of the congregation. We cut a large 3' x 5' rectangle from a piece of cardboard. We covered it with bright flame-colored paint and then randomly attached long flame colored streamers. We attached this entire "flaming panel" to a wire (streamers hanging down) so it could descend from the balcony to the chancel, passing the long "flames" over the heads of the congregation.

Prayers of the People

We tied a cluster of white helium balloons to the altar rail. Before the Prayers, a youth untied the cluster, sat on the floor, and as the prayers were read, released a single balloon at a time.

WIND

BULLETIN

PRELUDE

We invite you to consider the following passage while listening to the music of the Prelude. Reading is from Psalm 135, verse 7:

> He it is who makes the clouds rise at the end of the earth;
>
> > he makes lightning for the rain
> >
> > > and brings out the wind from his storehouses.

WORDS OF WELCOME

CALL TO WORSHIP

*PROCESSIONAL HYMN

"All Creatures of Our God and King"
> *Geistliche Kirchengesäng, 1623*

*UNISON PRAYER OF CONFESSION

Congregation
> Dear Lord, we hear the words of the prophet Jeremiah in Jeremiah 5:12–13: They have spoken falsely of the LORD, and have said, "He will do nothing. No evil will come upon us, and we shall not see sword or famine" . . . *(stop and breathe)*
>
> "The prophets are nothing but wind, for the word is not in them. Thus shall it be done to them!" . . . *(stop and breathe)*
>
> We confess that we have heard the words but we have not listened . . . *(stop and breathe)*
>
> We listen to false prophets; we speak falsely ourselves . . . *(stop and breathe)*
>
> Open our hearts, our minds, and cleanse us . . . *(stop and breathe)*
>
> We ask this in the name of Jesus Christ. Amen.

ASSURANCE

*GLORIA PATRI

TIME WITH ADULTS

Job 27:19–23

OLD TESTAMENT READING

Exodus 14:21–22 and 15:9–10

NEW TESTAMENT READING

Mark 4:35–41

MEDITATIONS

Part I: Invites and Destroys

Part II: Power and Nothingness

*HYMN

"How Great Thou Art"
Swedish folk melody

Part III: Beginnings and Ends

*HYMN

"Wind Who Makes All Winds That Blow"
Joseph Parry, 1879

CALL TO OFFERING

*THE DOXOLOGY

*RECEIVING OF THE OFFERING

*HYMN

"Every Time I Feel the Spirit"
African-American spiritual

PRAYERS OF THE PEOPLE AND THE YOUTH

THE LORD'S PRAYER

*CLOSING HYMN

"Breathe on Me, Breath of God"
Robert Jackson, 1894

*BENEDICTION

Youth
> And now go forth into the world filled with the rush of the Spirit of God and in peace.

Congregation
> Together may we share the light of God's countenance upon us. May the Lord bless you, children, and keep you.

Youth

And may the Lord bless you, too, O Children of God.

* CHORAL BENEDICTION

"Irish Benediction"

POSTLUDE

*Those who are able, please stand.

BLOOD

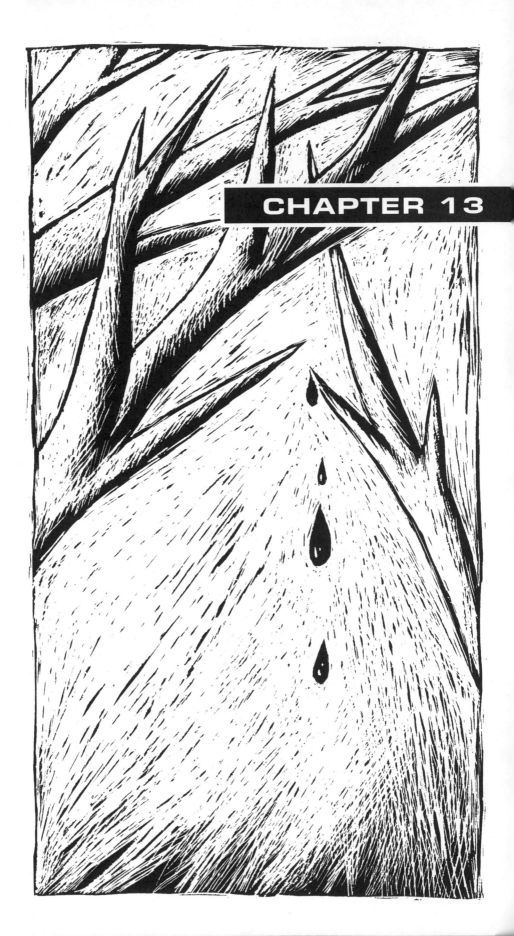

CHAPTER 13

PRELUDE

We invite you to consider the following passages while listening to the music of the Prelude. Readings are from Genesis 49, and Revelation 14, verses 19 and 20:

. . . he washes his garments in wine

and his robe in the blood of grapes.

(Genesis 49:11b)

So the angel swung his sickle over the earth and gathered the vintage of the earth, and he threw it into the great wine press of the wrath of God. And the wine press was trodden outside the city, and blood flowed from the wine press, as high as a horse's bridle, for a distance of about two hundred miles (Revelation 14:19–20).

BLOOD[1]

WORDS OF WELCOME

Youth 1 (lectern)

The youth of _____ Church of _____ welcome you to this special time during which the young people of the church plan and lead our worship.

Youth 2 (pulpit)

Today our worship time will revolve around the theme of blood. We chose this because of its symbolic power in our Christian theology.

Youth 1

We also see blood more literally as a life-giving and a life-threatening matter in our modern world. We think of those who need blood. We think of those who have infected blood. We think of those who shed blood.

Youth 2

We invite you to join in the spirit of our worship today. As youth in this congregation, it is a privilege to prepare this service, and it is our gift to you.

CALL TO WORSHIP

Youth 3 (back of sanctuary)

As we hear from Psalm 9, verse 11: Sing praises to the LORD, who dwells in Zion. Declare his deeds among the peoples. For he who avenges blood is mindful of them; he does not forget the cry of the afflicted.

---

1. This service was a particular challenge because it was scheduled for the First Sunday of Lent and included Communion as well as two offerings. The entire service is included here, but it may be necessary to eliminate sections in the interests of time.

*PROCESSIONAL HYMN

"O Love, How Deep, How Broad, How High"
    "The Agincourt Song," England, c. 1415

*RESPONSIVE READING

Youth 4 (lectern)

Let us join in the Responsive Reading from Proverbs 1:8–11 and 15–19 as written in your bulletins.

Youth (in unison)

Hear, my child, your father's instruction, and do not reject your mother's teaching; for they are a fair garland for your head, and pendants for your neck.

Congregation

My child if sinners entice you, do not consent. If they say, "Come with us, let us lie in wait for blood; let us wantonly ambush the innocent . . ."

Youth

My child, do not walk in their way, keep your foot from their paths; for their feet run to evil, and they hurry to shed blood. For in vain is the net baited while the bird is looking on; yet they lie in wait—to kill themselves! and set an ambush—for their own lives!

Unison

Such is the end of all who are greedy for gain; it takes away the life of its possessors.

*GLORIA PATRI

TIME WITH ADULTS

The Story of Sibling Rivalry (Genesis 37:17b–34)

Youth 5 (lectern)

Usually there is a special time for children in the service during which the children hear a Bible story or a simple lesson. In our service today, we, the children, will tell you a story, the story from Genesis of Joseph, his coat, and his brothers.

Youth 6 (pulpit)

So Joseph went after his brothers, and found them at Dothan. They saw him from a distance, and before he came near to them, they conspired to kill him. They said to one another, "Here comes this dreamer. Come now, let us kill him and throw him into one of the pits;

---

*Those who are able to stand should do so for each part of the service marked with an asterisk.

Youth 7 stands and gestures toward the "pit."

Youth 6

then we shall say that a wild animal has devoured him, and we shall see what will become of his dreams." But when Reuben heard it, he delivered him out of their hands, saying, "Let us not take his life." Reuben said to them, "Shed no blood; throw him into this pit here in the wilderness, but lay no hand upon him"—that he might rescue him out of their hand and restore him to his father.

Youth 8 (Reuben) stands up and gestures. He then leaves by a side door.

Youth 6

So when Joseph came to his brothers, they stripped him of his robe, the long robe with sleeves that he wore; and they took him and threw him into a pit. The pit was empty; there was no water in it. Then they sat down to eat;

Youth 9 (Joseph) walks slowly down the aisle during this last reading. When he arrives at the front, Youths 9, 10, 11, 12 (brothers) grab him, tear off his robe, and cast him into the "pit." Youths 13, 14, 15, 16 (Ishmaelites) enter from a side door in a line as if a "caravan."

Youth 6

and looking up they saw a caravan of Ishmaelites coming from Gilead, with their camels carrying gum, balm, and resin, on their way to carry it down to Egypt.

The brothers act as if they are talking together while pointing to caravan.

Youth 6

Then Judah said to his brothers, "What profit is it if we kill our brother and conceal his blood? Come, let us sell him to the Ishmaelites, and not lay our hands on him, for he is our brother, our own flesh." And his brothers agreed.

When some Midianite traders passed by, they drew Joseph up, lifting him out of the pit, and sold him to the Ishmaelites for twenty pieces of silver. And they took Joseph to Egypt.

The brothers pull Joseph out of "pit," and trade him to the Ishmaelites for money.

Youth 6

When Reuben returned to the pit and saw that Joseph was not in the pit, he tore his clothes. He returned to his brothers, and said, "The boy is gone; and I, where can I turn?"

Reuben reenters from the side door and looks into the "pit." The brothers take robe, turning it inside out so you can see "blood."

Youth 6

Then they took Joseph's robe, slaughtered a goat, and dipped the robe in the blood;

The brothers carry the robe down aisle to Youth 17 (Jacob), who is seated midway. When he sees the robe, he stands and gestures his despair as he walks out the back.

Youth 6

They had the long robe with sleeves taken to their father, and they said, "This we have found; see now whether it is your son's robe or not." He recognized it, and said, "It is my son's robe! A wild animal has devoured him; Joseph is without doubt torn to pieces." Then Jacob tore his garments, and put sackcloth on his loins, and mourned for his son many days.

* HYMN

"I'm Gonna Live So God Can Use Me"
African-American spiritual

Joseph goes to the front and raises hands high, directs the congregation, turns to face the altar, and generally acts enthusiastic.

THE FIRST OLD TESTAMENT READING

Youth 18 (pulpit)

We begin our Scripture lesson today with a story of blood that protects Israel. This is the ancient story of the Passover, in which blood is the sign to God of the faithfulness of his people and his commitment to protect them. Hear, now, the reading.

Youth 19 (lectern)

The Old Testament Reading today is from Exodus 12, verses 1–3, 6–7, 12–13.

During the reading Youths 20 and 21 drape the tops of the sanctuary side doors with long strips of red crepe paper.

The LORD said to Moses and Aaron in the land of Egypt: This month shall mark for you the beginning of months; it shall be the first month of the year for you. Tell the whole congregation of Israel that on the tenth of this month they are to take a lamb for each family, a lamb for each household.

You shall keep it until the fourteenth day of this month; then the whole assembled congregation of Israel shall slaughter it at twilight. They shall take some of the blood and put it on the two doorposts and the lintel of the houses in which they eat it.

For I will pass through the land of Egypt that night, and I will strike down every firstborn in the land of Egypt, both human beings and animals; on all the gods of Egypt I will execute judgments: I am the LORD. The blood shall be a sign for you on the houses where you live: when I see the blood, I will pass over you, and no plague shall destroy you when I strike the land of Egypt.

THE SECOND OLD TESTAMENT READING

Youth 18 (pulpit)

But blood does not always mean safety. In fact, the sign of blood can mean ostracism, discrimination, separation from each other. Rather than unite us as a people of God, blood was a sign that some were unclean. Hear these harsh laws as read to us from Leviticus.

Youths 22 and 23 (both girls) read into a microphone from behind the backdrop where they cannot be seen. Read in very loud and harsh tones:

The Second Old Testament Reading for today is from Leviticus 15, verses 19–21.

When a woman has a discharge of blood that is her regular discharge from her body, she shall be in her impurity for seven days, and whoever touches her shall be unclean until the evening. Everything upon which she lies during her impurity shall be unclean; everything also upon which she sits shall be unclean. Whoever touches her bed shall wash his clothes, and bathe in water, and be unclean until the evening.

Youth 18

We, too, live in a world where people are ostracized, segregated, and outcast because of their blood. People with HIV and AIDS are also treated as unclean, as people to be denied certain rights, certain care, and understanding.

Let me ask who in the congregation received red bulletins when you arrived today. Can you raise your hand with the bulletin, please. *(Wait)* I need the help of those who have the red bulletins.

To remind us of the pain of such segregation, could you bring your bulletins and come forward to the front of the sanctuary. Please stand over here behind this screen in front of the lectern. *(Wait)*

(To people in congregation): This is how people are isolated and pronounced unclean. They are labeled, they are segregated, they are considered unclean.

(To people in corral): Please stay there and listen to the New Testament Reading.

THE NEW TESTAMENT READING

Youth 18

But I say to you now, in Jesus Christ we find a new way. In this New Testament reading, Christ frees us from the horror of separation and judgment. In it the love of Christ overcomes all labels, all divisions, all corrals, and all condemnations.

Youth 24 (lectern)

The New Testament Reading is from Mark 5:25–34.

Now there was a woman who had been suffering from hemorrhages for twelve years. She had endured much under many physicians, and had spent all that she had; and she was no better, but rather grew worse. She had heard about Jesus, and came up behind him in the crowd and touched his cloak, for she said, "If I but touch his clothes, I will be made well." Immediately her hemorrhage stopped; and she felt in her body that she was healed of her disease. Immediately aware that power had gone forth from him, Jesus turned about in the crowd and said, "Who touched my clothes?" And his disciples said to him, "You see the crowd pressing in on you; how can you say, 'Who touched me?' " He looked all around to see who had done it. But the woman, knowing what had happened to her, came in fear and trembling, fell down before him, and told him the whole truth. He said to her, "Daughter, your faith has made you well; go in peace, and be healed of your disease."

Youth 18

In Jesus Christ we find a new way. To those in the group with the red bulletins, thank you, and you may now return to your seats. We are reunited in our faith and in the love of Christ.

*HYMN

"Every Time I Feel the Spirit"
African-American spiritual

CALL TO OFFERING

Youth 25

It is through our giving and our commitment that we can truly live up to the challenges of our faith. As Proverbs 12, verses 2 and 6, state: The good obtain favor from the Lord, but those who devise evil he condemns. The words of the wicked are a deadly ambush, but the speech of the upright delivers them. The wicked are overthrown and are no more, but the house of the righteous will stand. *(Hand offering plates to the ushers.)*

OFFERTORY

*THE DOXOLOGY

*RECEIVING OF THE OFFERING

Youth 25 (front of sanctuary as she takes the offering plates from ushers):
My hope is built on nothing less

Than Jesus' blood and righteousness;

I dare not trust the sweetest frame,

But wholly lean on Jesus' name.

MEDITATIONS

Part I: Blood, Wasted

Youth 26 (pulpit)

For the first part of our Meditation this morning we turn our attention to those whose blood has been wasted. We remember those who have suffered violence and those who are no longer with us, the result of violent deaths. We yearn for peace, yet our world still encompasses violence. As we read the names of those we have lost, let us join in the song of farewell.

HYMN OF FAREWELL

"Shalom, Chaverim! Farewell, Good Friends"

Israeli round

During the singing, Youth 26 reads a list into a microphone of those who are victims of violence so it can be heard over the singing.

Part II: Blood, the Sacrifice for Us All

THE LORD'S SUPPER

Invitation to the Lord's Table

Youth 27

Jesus said:

Behold, I stand at the door and knock;

if those who hear my voice open the door,

I will come in to them and eat with them,

and they with me.

O taste and see that the Lord is good!

Happy are all who find refuge in God![2]

Great Thanksgiving

Youth 27

With thanksgiving, let us offer God our grateful praise. Please rise.

The Lord be with you

Congregation

And also with you.

Youth 28

Lift up your hearts.

---

2. Liturgy taken from *Book of Common Worship* (Louisville, KY: Westminster/John Knox Press, 1993): p. 125. Reprinted by permission.

Congregation

We lift them to the Lord.

Youth 28

Let us give thanks to the Lord our God.

Congregation

It is right to give our thanks and praise.

Youth 28

Let us pray.

Holy God, Father almighty, Creator of heaven and earth,

with joy we praise you and give thanks to your name.

You commanded light to shine out of darkness,

divided the sea and dry land,

created the vast universe and called it good.

You made us in your image to live with one another in love.

You gave us the breath of life

and freedom to choose your way.

You promised yourself in covenant with Abraham and Sarah,

told us your purpose in commandments through Moses,

and called for justice in the cry of prophets.

Through long generations

you have been faithful and kind to all your children. Amen.[3]

Great Thanksgiving: Words of Institution

Youth 27

Please be seated. *(Wait)* Hear the words of the institution of the Holy Supper of our Lord Jesus Christ:

Youth 28

We give you thanks

that on the night of his arrest,

Jesus took bread,

and after giving thanks to God,

he broke it, and gave it to his disciples, saying: Take, eat.

This is my body, given for you.

Do this in remembrance of me.

---

3. From *Book of Common Worship*, p. 130.

Youth 27

In the same way he took the cup, saying:

This cup is the covenant sealed in my blood,

shed for you for the forgiveness of sins.

Whenever you drink it,

do this in remembrance of me.[4]

Youth 28

Every time you eat this bread and drink this cup, you proclaim the saving death of the risen Lord, until he comes.

Great Thanksgiving: Blessing

The Minister

Merciful God,

by your Holy Spirit bless and make holy

both us and these your gifts of bread and wine,

that the bread we break may be communion in the body of Christ,

and the cup we bless may be a communion in the blood of Christ.

Here we offer ourselves to be a living sacrifice,

holy and acceptable to you.

In your mercy, accept this our sacrifice of praise and thanksgiving,

as, in communion with all the faithful in heaven and on earth,

we ask you to fulfill, in us and in all creation,

the purpose of your redeeming love.

Through Christ, with Christ, in Christ,

in the unity of the Holy Spirit,

all glory and honor are yours, almighty God,

now and forever. Amen.[5]

We now invite you to come forward and receive the Lord's Supper. The ushers will indicate the best order. If you wish to remain in your seat and receive communion there, please indicate this to the usher.

Communion Hymn

"Let Us Break Bread Together"

African-American spiritual

---

4. From *Book of Common Worship*, p. 154.

5. From *Book of Common Worship*, p. 141.

Prayer of Dedication

Youth 28

Let us bow our heads for the Prayer of Dedication:

Almighty God,

you provide the true bread from heaven,

your Son, Jesus Christ our Lord.

Grant that we who have received the Sacrament of his body and blood

may abide in him and he in us,

that we may be filled with the power of his endless life,

now and forever. Amen.[6]

Part III: Blood, the Life Giver Today (Optional)

Youth 29 (pulpit)

The third part of our Meditation moves us to the way we as individuals can make the gift of blood to someone else. We will now pass out two items. The first are Lifesavers.

Youth 30 (lectern)

Lifesavers! What a silly thing to hand out in church.

Youth 29

Not at all. Lifesavers are great symbols. First they are red and white, symbolizing the red and white corpuscles in our blood.

Youth 31 (from mid aisle)

Second, they are round, the symbol of eternity, the symbol of the alpha and the omega, the beginning and the end.

Youth 29

And, of course, they are life savers in a real way because with them comes a pledge card. We ask any of you who are able to sign your name to this pledge card and hand it in during the special offering. By doing so you are promising that within the month you will visit a blood bank and donate blood.

Youth 31

We will now collect a special offering. Your gifts in this offering will be donated to the Red Cross, and we ask that you also send in the pledge card if you can commit to a blood donation within the next month.

ANTHEM

"Come, Let Us Eat"
Billema Kwillia; arranged by Robert Rhein

---

6. From *Book of Common Worship*, p. 158.

Note: Because of the length of the service, do not bring the offering forward after it is collected.

PRAYERS OF THE PEOPLE

Youth 32 (lectern)

Let us bow now for prayer.

Dear Lord, we begin our prayers today full of the warmth and life that you have given us.

We remember today and give thanks for the many scientists and doctors and nurses and students who have contributed to our understanding of our blood systems and our health. We remember particularly the great African American scientist, Charles Drew, who led the way in our understanding of plasma and who created the first blood banks, yet who, himself, was not given medical attention in a white hospital following an automobile accident solely because of ignorance and prejudice regarding his race. Ironically, he was denied an immediate blood transfusion needed to save his life.

We remember too, today, those who shed blood. We remember those who gave of themselves that others might have freedom and safety. We also remember those who died unnecessary deaths, victims of the irrational violence and random attacks that seem to occur all around us and our larger world.

We pray today for those in poor health, those with chronic diseases of the blood, those with phlebitis, leukemia, hemophilia, AIDS and HIV. Be with them as they struggle with pain and limitations, fear and anxiety, loneliness, and, at times, misunderstanding. Help all of us to find it in our hearts and schedules to reach out, comfort, and support them.

We give thanks today for the huge gift you have given us in our Christianity. Thank you for the great symbols of the church, the powerful Sacraments, the unfolding challenges to seek a better life within your kingdom.

Be with us in all these times, and remind us constantly of Jesus Christ, who taught us to pray . . .

THE LORD'S PRAYER

Our Father, who art in heaven . . .

*CLOSING HYMN

"My Hope Is Built on Nothing Less"
William B. Bradbury, 1863

*BENEDICTION

Youth (gathered at the chancel steps)

And now go forth into the world in health, in peace, and in grace.

Congregation

Together may we share the light of God's countenance upon us. May God bless you, children, and keep you.

Youth

And may God bless you, too, O Children of God.

POSTLUDE

The following is a list and description of the things needed in the service. We have organized them by the order required.

Backdrop

We painted our backdrop a deep red.

Dress Code

Each participant in the service wore red clothing (except when in costume).

BLOOD

If a youth had nothing red, we allowed black or white.

Pew Pledge Cards (Optional)

We requested pledge cards from the session and received permission for a special offering to be taken during this service. The offering was for funds to go to the Red Cross. It also was a chance for people to pledge to give blood at a local blood drive. The pledge cards were simple pink index cards with red borders, asking for names and phone numbers.

Bulletins

We printed about twenty-five bulletins on red paper. The rest were on regular white paper. The red bulletins were used in the Second Old Testament Reading.

Time with Adults

At two points in this particular service we needed a fenced-off space. The first was for the enactment of the Joseph story, during which Joseph is thrown into a pit. We set up a four-foot high panel perpendicular to a side wall to serve as a "pit." Later, in the Second Old Testament Reading, we asked all those holding red bulletins to come forward and stand behind the panel as if they were cast aside and segregated from the rest of the congregation.

The Joseph story required costumes. All participants wore various simple robes with colorful tie belts and headdresses. Joseph's robe included red strips of material pinned inside. The Ishmaelites carried riches (jewelry boxes, brass objects) and traded gold coins for Joseph.

First Old Testament Reading

Long strips of red crepe paper are hung with transparent tape on the doorposts.

Meditation: Part III—Blood, the Life Giver Today

We passed baskets of red and white Lifesavers. We also passed offering plates to collect the pledge cards that had been set out on the pews (see section above on Time with Adults).

BLOOD

BULLETIN

PRELUDE

We invite you to consider the following passages while listening to the music of the Prelude. Readings are from Genesis 49, verse 11, and Revelation 14, verses 19 and 20:

> . . . he washes his garments in wine
>
> and his robe in the blood of grapes.
>
> (Genesis 49:11b)

> So the angel swung his sickle over the earth and gathered the vintage of the earth, and he threw it into the great wine press of the wrath of God. And the wine press was trodden outside the city, and blood flowed from the wine press, as high as a horse's bridle, for a distance of about two hundred miles.
>
> (Revelation 14:19–20)

WORDS OF WELCOME

CALL TO WORSHIP

*PROCESSIONAL HYMN

"O Love, How Deep, How Broad, How High"
  "The Agincourt Song," England, c. 1415

*RESPONSIVE READING

Proverbs 1:8–11, 15–19

Youth
  Hear, my child, your father's instruction, and do not reject your mother's teaching; for they are a fair garland for your head, and pendants for your neck.

Congregation
  My child, if sinners entice you, do not consent. If they say, "Come with us, let us lie in wait for blood, let us wantonly ambush the innocent . . ."

Youth
  My child, do not walk in their way, keep your foot from their paths; for their feet run to evil, and they hurry to shed blood. For in vain is a net baited while the bird is looking on; yet they lie in wait—to kill themselves! and set an ambush for their own lives!

Unison
  Such is the end of all who are greedy for gain; it takes away the life of its possessors.

*GLORIA PATRI

TIME WITH ADULTS

The Story of Sibling Rivalry (Genesis 37:17b–34)

*HYMN

"I'm Gonna Live So God Can Use Me"
African-American spiritual

THE FIRST OLD TESTAMENT READING

Exodus 12:1–3, 6–7, 12–13

THE SECOND OLD TESTAMENT READING

Leviticus 15:19–21

THE NEW TESTAMENT READING

Mark 5:25–34

*HYMN

"Every Time I Feel the Spirit"
African-American spiritual

CALL TO OFFERING

OFFERTORY

*THE DOXOLOGY

*RECEIVING OF THE OFFERING

MEDITATIONS

Part I: Blood, Wasted

HYMN OF FAREWELL

"Shalom, Chaverim! Farewell, Good Friends"
Israeli round

Part II: Blood, the Sacrifice for Us All

THE LORD'S SUPPER

Invitation to the Lord's Supper

Great Thanksgiving

Youth

> With thanksgiving, let us offer God our grateful praise. Please rise.
>
> The Lord be with you.

Congregation

> And also with you.

Youth

> Lift up your hearts.

Congregation

> We lift them to the Lord.

Youth

> Let us give thanks to the Lord our God.

Congregation

> It is right to give our thanks and praise.

Youth

> Let us pray.
>
> Holy God, Father almighty, Creator of heaven and earth,
>
> with joy we praise you and give thanks to your name.
>
> You commanded light to shine out of darkness,
>
> divided the sea and dry land,
>
> created the vast universe and called it good.
>
> You made us in your image to live with one another in love.
>
> You gave us the breath of life and freedom to choose your way.
>
> You promised yourself in covenant with Abraham and Sarah,
>
> told us your purpose in commandments through Moses,
>
> and called for justice in the cry of prophets.
>
> Through long generations
>
> you have been faithful and kind to all your children. Amen.[7]

Great Thanksgiving: Words of Institution

Great Thanksgiving: Blessing

Communion Hymn

"Let Us Break Bread Together"
> *African-American spiritual*

---

7. From *Book of Common Worship*, p. 130.

Prayer of Dedication

Part III: Blood, the Life Giver Today

ANTHEM

"Come, Let Us Eat"
Billema Kwillia; arranged by Robert Rhein

PRAYERS OF THE PEOPLE

THE LORD'S PRAYER

*CLOSING HYMN

"My Hope Is Built on Nothing Less"
William B. Bradbury, 1863

*BENEDICTION

Youth

And now go forth into the world in health, in peace, and in grace.

Congregation

Together may we share the light of God's countenance upon us. May God bless you, children, and keep you.

Youth

And may God bless you, too, O Children of God.

POSTLUDE

*Those who are able, please stand.